Praise for *Young Money*

"This book is an amazing resource for those who are looking to get a head start on creating a foundation of financial literacy that will lead to an even brighter future for themselves and their families!"
—**Rennie Curran, author of *Free Agent* and professional athlete**

"Mr. Yarnway has managed to break down the complexities of building wealth into a step-by-step guide that is applicable to any investor."
—**Sean George, Executive Director and Partner, Berknell Financial Group**

"This timeless book is a rite of passage for every millennial investor."
—**Bishop K. R. Woods, Chairman, Northern California District Council**

"This book is as insightful as it is inspiring—a must-read for every millennial looking to acquire wealth."
—**Abhinav Mathur, CEO, Hulaloop**

"This book gives you the tools that should be taught in school. Grab this book to empower yourself!"
—**Jahvid Best, Olympic sprinter and professional football player**

"One of the best financial books I've read in a long time!"
—**Donovan Carter, actor, *Ballers*, HBO**

"Learning to be financially healthy at an early age is one of the most critical things one can do. Dasarte Yarnway's new book is a crucial primer for millennials, and more than a few Gen Xers like myself, on how to build a financial present and future that's stable and successful."
—**Lawrence Ross, *Los Angeles Times* bestselling author of *The Divine Nine***

"I now know why Dasarte is so highly regarded in the finance world. His knowledge combined with his prose makes a daunting idea such as wealth accumulation achievable for all. I highly recommend this book to all those in pursuit of achieving their financial goals."
—**Jeff Johnson, Principal, JIJ Communications; BET host; and award-winning journalist**

YOUNG
MONEY

YOUNG MONEY

4 Proven Actions to Design Your Wealth While You Still Can

DASARTE YARNWAY

Foreword by Pete Najarian, founder of Investitute and contributor to CNBC's *Fast Money*

BK

Berrett–Koehler Publishers, Inc.
a BK Life book

Berrett-Koehler Publishers, Inc.
1333 Broadway, Suite 1000
Oakland, CA 94612-1921
Tel: (510) 817-2277   Fax: (510) 817-2278   www.bkconnection.com

Ordering Information
Quantity sales. Special discounts are available on quantity purchases by corporations, associations, and others. For details, contact the "Special Sales Department" at the Berrett-Koehler address above.
Individual sales. Berrett-Koehler publications are available through most bookstores. They can also be ordered directly from Berrett-Koehler: Tel: (800) 929-2929; Fax: (802) 864-7626; www.bkconnection.com
Orders for college textbook/course adoption use. Please contact Berrett-Koehler: Tel: (800) 929-2929; Fax: (802) 864-7626.

Distributed to the U.S. trade and internationally by Penguin Random House Publisher Services.

Berrett-Koehler and the BK logo are registered trademarks of Berrett-Koehler Publishers, Inc.

Printed in the United States of America

Berrett-Koehler books are printed on long-lasting acid-free paper. When it is available, we choose paper that has been manufactured by environmentally responsible processes. These may include using trees grown in sustainable forests, incorporating recycled paper, minimizing chlorine in bleaching, or recycling the energy produced at the paper mill.

ISBN 978-1-5230-9216-1

Library of Congress Cataloging-in-Publication Data
Names: Yarnway, Dasarte, author.
Title: Young money : 4 proven actions to design your wealth while you still can / Dasarte Yarnway ; foreword by Pete Najarian.
Description: First Edition. | Oakland, CA : Berrett-Koehler Publishers, 2018.
Identifiers: LCCN 2017042705 | ISBN 9781523092161 (paperback)
Subjects: LCSH: Finance, Personal. | Saving and investment. | BISAC: BUSINESS & ECONOMICS / Personal Finance / Money Management. | BUSINESS & ECONOMICS / Motivational.
Classification: LCC HG179 .Y347 2018 | DDC 332.024/01--dc23
LC record available at https://lccn.loc.gov/2017042705

First Edition
25 24 23 22 21 20 19 18   10 9 8 7 6 5 4 3 2 1

Project management, design, and composition by Steven Hiatt, Hiatt & Dragon, San Francisco Copyeditor: Steven Hiatt Proofreader: Tom Hassett Cover designer: Rob Johnson, Toprotype Inc.

To Tinniziee for giving me a seat at the table.

Contents

Conclusion: Mastering Your Legacy

Foreword

Ever since I became an options trader back in 1992, I have seen the financial markets rise and fall dramatically, and with those movements the livelihoods and savings of people who knew some of the basics but none of the nuances and details of how markets work. However, I also noticed that a large segment of the population that had the most potential for profits and financial stability were also those who seemed least involved in investing: the younger generation.

There's perhaps good reason for this: The majority of the books and programming you see in the marketplace are geared toward older people with some assets and knowledge of the marketplace. It's easy to see why younger people would conclude that financial planning is just not for them. To someone just getting started in managing their own money, seeing someone talk about dividends, stocks, options, and other such items is overwhelming, and probably makes them feel like they are not in the right income bracket for such an education.

That's why this book is important—very important.

The fact is that all of us, no matter what our income and bank balance, need money management skills and knowledge, and younger people need it more than anyone else. While the financial literacy and education provided to young people remains virtually nonexistent, the mistakes they make that result in debt, poor credit, etc., will impact them adversely for the rest of their lives. Conversely, as Dasarte shows in this book, a good financial mindset early on will have a positive impact for the rest of their lives. The better the start a person has, the more time he or she has to slowly build real wealth.

"Real wealth" is an important thing to define. Real wealth is for the long term and is what provides that which is most important: stability and security. Unfortunately, the current popular mindset focuses on short-term gains and mistakes having a hefty checking account balance for security. As opportunities and markets become more limited and competition more aggressive, it gets easier to mistake momentary security for long-term stability.

The point this book makes better than most is that time is the greatest asset of all for building wealth. With time, you can experiment, explore various options, learn from mistakes, bounce back from setbacks, steadily and consistently build up wealth at a sustainable pace, and accumulate more assets and hence achieve greater security.

And time is the one thing that the younger generations have that no one else outside that group has nor can buy at any price. It is, quite frankly, the best tool there is when it comes to building financial security.

You always hear that common lament of "If I knew then what I know now...." Well, now, with this book, there are no excuses. You will now know everything and have enough time to use it. Get to it!

— Pete Najarian

INTRODUCTION

THE ULTIMATE ADVANTAGE

Time is your biggest asset—what you do with your time will determine how you leverage all the other assets in your life.

Time: Your
Most Valuable Asset

The Roaring Twenties were a memorable time in the United States and in world history. In the United States, there was a desire for innovation, creation, and risk-taking. This decade brought America exponential economic growth, fostered revered art and artists, philosophers, and social movements, and was brimming with transformation that could be felt from coast to coast.

Like the period of the Roaring Twenties in American history, your early professional years (roughly ages twenty to forty) are the most vibrant in your life. You are encouraged to explore the country, the world around you, and every possibility. You will experience the extremes of good and bad, and are young and energetic enough to surge forward with hope into the future. At this stage, you are filling your wealth bucket drip by drip, and anything you can do to shore up your financial situation will lead to exponentially greater assets down the line.

When it comes to designing your wealth, young people have the ultimate advantage: time. The time value of money principle suggests that a dollar today is worth more than a dollar tomorrow because of its appreciation potential and compounding of interest when invested. And the longer your money is put to work, the greater harvest you will reap. That is why time is the greatest asset you can possess. But it cannot be bought. You either have it or you don't, and if you're reading this book, you have it. Now here's how to make it work for you.

Four Simple Steps

For years, we, the professionals of the financial services industry, have failed young people (and their more mature counterparts, for that matter). We've muddied the waters of fundamental investing with jargon and ego-boosting hypotheses on what the market will do next. We've focused on how much better we can sound than the next guy—instead of thinking about how much better we can serve our clients. Our most serious error is that we've complicated the process of designing your wealth.

It took over a thousand prospective client meetings for me to "get" all the things that we were doing wrong. People didn't care about my smooth talk, all the fancy terminology I used, or even the tailored suits that I wore. What they cared about was creating money management plans that made sense for them now and that could grow with them and change with their circumstances, plans that would protect them from the blows life inevitably deals out and that would maximize their current and future fortunes. I realized that we had been wasting our time on the trivial things and not focusing on helping individuals really build out their unique visions of prosperity. And based on this realization, I developed a simple, four-step mastery approach to designing long-term wealth:

1. Master the Mindset.
2. Master the Plan.
3. Master Your Income.
4. Master Money Drains.

The Mastery Approach

Anyone can be a Master Wealth-Builder, but becoming one first starts with a decision, a decision to want to be better. Master Wealth-Builders are not born, they are made. They are you and me. They are our mothers and fathers. They are our grandparents, our teachers, physicians, law enforcement, entertainment professionals, politicians, athletes, and religious leaders. They are normal people who have committed to building upon whatever foundation they have inherited. They believe that they can take their thoughts and plans and manifest them into realities.

Today, we see Master Wealth-Builders on the grand stage of the media, idolized for their financial achievements. We see the spotlights, the big businesses, the assets, and all the things that we're led to believe mark success. What we don't see is the challenges they faced, the risks they took, and the mental fortitude they had to exhibit daily and relentlessly to get to that point.

When you're young, mastering wealth is primarily about mastering time—making each day that you have (and that you won't have tomorrow) work at maximum efficiency for you. Because mastery is built by repetition. You set up a plan, and then you work that plan to exhaustion until you've internalized your mission and every action you take is in service of it. You work diligently every single day to reach your ultimate goal. Mastery is synonymous with action, and action is the only thing that yields results. This is what it takes to build your wealth over the course of a lifetime (and beyond).

Being young is the ultimate advantage when it comes to mastering wealth, but this is not just a feel-good book about how you can leverage your youth to attain long-term financial success. It is an instruction guide to help you improve the everyday qualitative and quantitative metrics that will guide your wealth-generation journey beginning today and continuing on for the rest of your life.

But Wait, There's One More Thing

Why should you listen to me? It's not only because I run a growing wealth management firm and serve clients who have the same concerns as you. It is not only because I watched my parents master these four steps upon their arrival from war-torn Liberia to lay a foundation for my siblings and myself. It is certainly not the fact that I have failed repeatedly in my own attempts to build wealth (and picked myself back up every single time).

If there is one reason why you should take my advice, it is because I am right here on the journey with you. I am the living embodiment of this book, my own case study. And it is working for me.

So if you are ready to go on this journey with me, let's begin. The road to wealth awaits us.

STEP 1

MASTER
THE MINDSET

Set your mind on a
definite goal
and observe how
quickly the world
stands aside to
let you pass.

— Napoleon Hill,
Think and Grow Rich

1

When Cars Fly

As I walked into the investment firm in San Mateo, California, for my first official day of work after college, I was certain I would change the world. Instead, the experience working at that firm changed me.

It was a typical overcast morning in the Bay Area, and all the new recruits gathered in the firm's lobby to take a tour of the premises. "Welcome to your new home!" said the assistant as we prepared to circle the research floor. There were glass windows that enclosed equity traders and research analysts as they processed buy-and-sell orders for clients and the firm's various portfolio strategies. People were glued to their seats, attention split between four computer screens each that displayed graphs that looked as if they had no correlation or trend. I made it a point to look at all the other members of my cohort. Their faces couldn't hide their excitement at the amazing opportunity to work at this firm. And I thought to myself, "I don't know anything about this stuff."

Yes, I knew nothing about finance and investing. I had played football in college and was on the trajectory to be an NFL draft pick when I tore my ACL. Realizing that I needed a new career path (and fast!), I looked around to see what else I could excel at. With nothing but ambition in my tank, I had interviewed at the investment firm and been hired as an investment associate.

As the week proceeded, I absorbed all that I could about the stock market and financial planning. Basic things like the definition of a stock, how markets work, and the average returns of specific investments were routinely typed in my search engine. But although I was accumulating fundamental knowledge of the industry, I still lacked the tools that would enable me to apply it. I could not pinpoint why investors chose to invest in certain companies over others.

And more importantly, I could not explain how these decisions could help a person build the wealth that I too yearned to build. From my naïve perspective, the stock market was a gamble that involved taking high risks on your principal to receive a reward that may or may not be realized at an undisclosed future date. Part of me was asking myself, "Why take the risk?" But the other, more ambitious part of me refused to let the opportunity to learn pass me by. Besides, I was a first-generation American born in an impoverished neighborhood—I did not have much to lose. And so I rolled the dice.

Every month after my arrival, a new cohort arrived and toured the premises just as I had. About four months in, with only a slightly better understanding of wealth-building, I was joined by a new employee with a knack for investing. Let's call him John. I observed John closely as he started his computer and organized his desk. His face was as tired as if he had been working for thirty years. He dressed conservatively, even more so than the standard for the financial services industry. He read voraciously and had a laser focus when it came to completing tasks.

When the day came for our first Q&A session with the firm's chief executive officer and billionaire investor, John proceeded to ask questions that many of us new hires could not even comprehend. The topic of the meeting centered on the correlation between investing and wealth-building, and my head was swimming with fundamental questions about how I, a kid from the inner city, could make my money work for me and build wealth. As the presentation progressed, many of the company's strategies and ways of analysis were explained. And although most of my cohorts were wide-eyed and clueless, there was one person who wasn't.

From the accumulation of wealth to the compound interest of dividends to the analysis of a company's financial position before investing in it, it seemed as if there was nothing that John did not know. He even hurled back tough questions at our billionaire CEO until the leader asked to see him after the meeting. I was thoroughly impressed and felt the need to follow up with John. I machine-gunned a million questions at him about wealth-building, stocks, and analysis. But my simplest question is the one that yielded the most important answer. I asked, "How do you know what to invest in?"

He turned slowly, looked at me dead in the eye, and replied, "I'm investing for the day when cars fly."

Wealth-Building Is a Marathon

There is an old adage that reminds us, "Life is a marathon and not a sprint." In a sprint, the runner sets her sights on a destination that is close in distance with a foreseeable end. When the starting gun is shot, the sprinter is eager to reach her top speed as soon as possible so that she can win the race. She exerts all her energy early because of the short-term nature of the competition.

But if, like John, your eyes are set far into the future to the day when cars fly, the race is anything but short-term. It is most certainly a marathon. In a marathon, a number of factors contribute to the success of the runner. The runner must breathe properly and keep her composure. She must assess the distance between her current position and her goal, but also be aware of the other competitors and of other risks, all while being disciplined enough to know when to kick it up a notch and make a pass. The marathon runner's mindset is one of consistency. It is the mindset that is routinely present in Master Wealth-Builders everywhere.

It is the mental shift from sprint to marathon that allows Master Wealth-Builders to stay committed to their goals. They know the road will be long and arduous, that many parts of the race must simply be endured, and that nothing worthwhile has ever come from comfort zones. They know that while their youth is an advantage, it also means that the journey will be that much longer, and that consistency over time is that much more important. They know how to master their mindsets to keep on going.

The bottom line is that wealth-building is a long-term goal and that young people like yourself have the longest term in which to do it right.

Thinking Counterintuitively

For many of us, our actions—in terms of wealth-building and otherwise—are emotionally driven and not based on rational conclusions. For example, a man plays the lottery and wins a few million dollars. Because his financial circumstances have changed overnight, all of the wealth-building work he had committed to prior to hitting the lotto are now, to him, unnecessary. "I'm rich!" he thinks to himself, which is the intuitive thing to feel. In truth, his winnings are a small deal in the grand scheme of Master Wealth-Building.

Let's take that scenario and apply some counterintuitive thinking. Instead of splurging on goods, the winner reassesses his current financial circumstances, where he would like to go, and how long it will take him to get there. He deliberates thoughtfully on all his options to make sure that his next course of action is logical, precise, and aligned with his plan. This is a hard thing to do. Ignoring our reactive intuition is extremely difficult. Yet restraining yourself from acting on impulse often yields the best rewards. Take the most recent stock market crash.

On September 29, 2008, the Dow Jones Industrial Average fell 778 points—the largest single-day drop in its history at the time. During the previous period, the stock market had been yielding generous returns year over year. Without much research or professional help, families could throw a dart at any stock or mutual fund and that investment had a high likelihood of appreciating in value. This steady growth and wealth accumulation made Americans greedy and overly confident in their abilities to invest. They strayed from their financial plans (if they had any to begin with) and had astronomical expectations for their portfolios.

Unlike the crash during the Great Depression, which took several years for the market to reach its all-time lows, the financial crisis of 2008 took just eighteen months for the market's value to drop by over 50 percent. Imagine investing $10,000 and waking up eighteen months later to just a little north of $5,000. Yikes! This was the same sentiment that most Americans had at the time. The thing that most Americans didn't do was to think counterintuitively about the current situation, which led to hundreds of billions of unrecoverable dollars lost.

Think about it: Your account value is now at approximately $5,000. You've suffered the emotional heartache of watching the markets dive over a relatively short time period. At this point, you've sworn to yourself that you'll never try this investing thing ever again. But, as Rothschild, an eighteenth-century banker, is said to have remarked, reaffirming the value of counterintuitive thinking, "The time to buy is when there is blood in the streets."

With the S&P 500 Index sitting at roughly 676 points, indeed, blood was in the streets. And so you make an unnatural, probably uncomfortable, and definitely counterintuitive decision. Instead of pulling your money out of the market, you invest another $10,000, giving you a grand total of 15 shares in the S&P 500 Index. Nine years later, the S&P 500 stands at 2,351. Those 15 shares that you purchased at the bottom of the financial crisis—and against your own intuition—are now worth more than $25,000!

Wealth is not an accident, nor does it happen with luck. Even if you win the lottery, the likelihood of keeping that newfound wealth is statistically slim to none without your making the mental shift to adopt a mindset of wealth-building. And make no mistake about it: Mastering your mindset is by far the hardest part of building long-term wealth. Wealth starts in your mind, and then it manifests in your life. Wealth is built every day through sacrifice and extremely intentional actions. But without mastering your own thoughts, wealth-building is impossible. Your thoughts are the cogs in the engine that drive you down the path toward wealth.

If you can focus on the bigger picture, way into the future to when cars fly, thinking counterintuitively will eventually become second nature. Luckily, your youth gives you plenty of time to build the required muscle memory and to make the right decisions that will positively impact your near- and long-term financial circumstances.

4 A.M. Faith

As a young student-athlete at the University of California, Berkeley, I had the privilege of sitting next to some of the world's best students and taking classes from some of the most brilliant professors. Students from all over the world convened in classrooms to share perspectives about life, race relations, business, and politics. The vast array of ideologies exposed me to different ways of thinking and disparities between communities and introduced me to concepts that I had never heard of before I enrolled.

The university's character, charm, and freethinking spirit helped me harness the power of thought and focus, a priceless skill that has allowed many of my fellow students to become pioneers and innovators in their respective industries after college. But for me, the biggest gift I received from Berkeley was the gift of observation, specifically, the opportunity to observe a truly fine gentleman: Ron Gould, associate head coach and running backs coach.

If you read Coach Gould's list of accomplishments, you'll learn that he is the father of "Running Back U" and played a big role in launching the collegiate careers of some of the best college football running backs in the history of the game. His observant yet disciplinarian style was aligned with his mission to develop boys into men and into better citizens, and it was evident in every single one of his actions on and off the field. As a player, I felt that Coach Gould knew everything about me. He was everywhere, all the time, and would do anything for the players that he coached. The one thing that he did not know was that I studied him just as much as he may have been studying me. This is how he taught me the value of 4 a.m. faith.

It is said that faith is the unwavering belief in what is not seen. Well then, 4 a.m. faith is the ability to *act* on what is not seen. It means doing the things necessary to work toward tangible results, fueled by what you believe. It brings life to faith, moving you closer each day to your goals. It is what you need to *do* to be successful in sports, wealth creation, and life in general.

Professionally, a goal of Coach G's was to be a head football coach for an organization so that he could continue to impact the lives of young men across the country. This was quite a lofty goal, considering the possibility of becoming head coach at Cal Berkeley was very slim. A personal goal of his was to remain in good physical shape so that he could be productive on and off the field and give his players and family the best of him.

Every morning at 4 a.m., Coach Gould took a walk before beginning his day. During this walk, he would meditate on the problems that he was facing, the things that he wanted to come to fruition, and the health and well-being of his family and players. He used the time to fuel his tank so that once his day began he could *take action* on all of the things that he wanted to manifest in his personal and professional life. After his walk, he would watch film to know what to coach on, and he could always be found in the weight room long before any of the other coaches and players were in the facility. He coached as if every day were an audition for his dream job.

In the spring of 2013, after the Cal football team went 5–7, the entire coaching staff was fired, including Coach Gould. But because of his 4 a.m. faith, I knew that Coach G's coaching career was far from over. Sure enough, a few weeks after being released from the California football staff, he was hired in grand fashion to be the head coach of a college football program in Northern California.

This is what happens when you operate with 4 a.m. faith! In the darkest hours, when everyone was still asleep, Coach Gould was taking the time to think about his goals, assess his plan from all angles, and determine the right course of action that would bring him one day closer to success. He worked relentlessly for what he wanted, even when it didn't seem possible that it could come to fruition. He coached every day with tenacity, passion, and belief, as if the job was right around the corner. And then it was.

Doubling Down

Life is just as volatile as the stock market or real estate market. We get married, we divorce. We purchase homes, we move. We lose jobs, we start new ones. We expand our families, we lose close loved ones, we inherit assets. The economy shifts and changes our perspective on our own goals. We get older. Life happens.

Life was what happened to Coach Gould when he got fired. And while not a betting man, he chose this moment, his lowest moment, to double down on his goals. There's counterintuitive thinking at its best! He was prepared. He put his 4 a.m. faith into action and it paid off.

Coach Gould's 4 a.m. faith and desire for a specific outcome was so strong that he was unmoved by hardship. He taught me that you have to double down on your dreams even when—*especially* when—your emotions tell you not to. Hardship acts as the signal for maximum exertion. It becomes the driver for premium gains. Master Wealth-Builders understand this best, then put their actions and money where their mouths are.

Five Key Habits of Master Wealth-Builders

When it comes to building long-term wealth, success first starts with a shift in mentality toward believing we can achieve an insurmountable task. We think it, we visualize it, we believe in it. And then, with 4 a.m. faith, we go one step further: We act on it—every day and in every intentional way, even in moments when we can't clearly see the destination. It is important to remember that wealth-building and financial plans are only words on paper; your behavior is the air that gives these words life. Four a.m. faith without work is dead. Your shift in thought must lead to a shift in habits if it's going to lead to wealth. Coach Gould mastered the mindset *and* the habits that led to his achieving his goals. And in this section, I explain how you can too.

The days of the successful person being the loud, outspoken, charismatic leader are over. They fooled you. None of those characteristics are prerequisites for building the wealth that you desire. However, there are five habits that I have found all Master Wealth-Builders engage in as a result of mastering their mindsets. These habits are what help people transform themselves from idle dreamers into Master Wealth-Builders:

1. Focus on the process.
2. Prioritize productivity.
3. Emphasize continuous learning.
4. Nurture your relationships.
5. Put yourself in the seat.

Habit #1: Focus on the process

There is one thing that you have to come to terms with when it comes to building your wealth: It takes time. Nothing worth having will be easy, and, as they say, nothing easy is really worth having. Rather than focusing on the end goal, focus your mental energy on the daily actions it will take to get from point A to point Z. You have to win the day! This habit is the most important one, because it fuels all the others.

There will be times where there is nothing that you can do to make your plan come to fruition faster, especially in relation to money management. (But at least take joy in the fact that by starting young you will get there much faster than if you started ten years from now!) You have to let time take its course and be steadfast in your endeavor. You have to master time in order to master wealth-building. You have to think long-term.

By focusing on the process and the bigger picture, you will learn to count the small victories. You will learn to see the lessons in the losses. Each time you take a wrong turn in the process, you will store that memory as valuable data for when a similar situation next arises. You will learn not to be discouraged; instead, you will be motivated to do better. If you aren't learning, you are not trying. If you're not trying, you are certainly not building.

The last facet of focusing on the process is doing the work. One of the greatest events in the world of sports is the Olympics. Every four years, the world's greatest athletes meet in a city to celebrate a diverse array of sports and to compete to be the best in the world. The truth is, the races and competitions are won long before the athletes descend onto the track, largely through the tireless training they've completed in the years preceding the competition.

Wealth-building, just like winning a gold medal, takes work and preparation—work that often is not very enjoyable but that is mandatory for a desired outcome. The mistake that most people make is using income for all other purposes except for wealth-building. With this line of action, there is no other outcome but the need to work for more income. We see it all the time.

Without discipline and hard work, the universe won't move out of your way to bring your goals closer to you. The work is the small victory. Your eventual success is validation that you have, indeed, done the work. It's so simple, but we make it complex. By inching forward day by day, you'll slowly but surely reach your desired destination.

Habit #2: Prioritize productivity

It is not enough just to be busy. Doing a million things with slapdash effort will yield one million haphazard results. That's not productivity; it's busyness.

Your plate is inevitably full. There are many things that will distract you from your goals. And your time, though your biggest asset, is still limited. So instead of taking this scatter-gun approach to the goals that you have set yourself, consider what you really want to get done and focus intently on those things.

Productivity means using your time wisely to further your goals. Furthermore, it is about giving your body the necessary fuel, in terms of nutrition and maintenance, so that you can keep pace in this marathon endeavor. Prioritizing productivity means changing your lifestyle so that you can maximize your time. By fertilizing your dreams with focus, your work will bear more fruit and increase your chances for spiritual, physical, and financial wealth. How efficient you are with production is your key to a more fruitful life. Don't talk about all of the things you want to achieve; be about it. Goals are reached by *doing*.

Go now and go often. You'll get much further than you think.

Habit #3: Emphasize continuous learning

The world is constantly changing. Every day there are new developments in your profession, the capital markets, and technology that could impact what you are trying to build. New knowledge helps you to adapt your plan to changing conditions. Know what you want out of your plan and learn what it takes to get it—today and for the day when cars fly. Commit to being a lifelong learner.

Habit #4: Nurture your relationships

Nurturing your relationships has more to do with what you can give than what others can give to you. And the relationships I'm referring to here are not only your professional ones, but also your family, friends, and the people who make up your inner circle. Building enduring wealth can sometimes take a village, and so it has to be about more than yourself and your immediate needs. Pouring energy into your relationships with the people you trust and admire and who make your life worth living will generate support for your plans and will help to reap the greatest rewards.

Habit #5: Put yourself in the seat

For as long as I can remember, I have imagined myself in the position that I find myself in now. There was no proof that I was going to build a company, help the people that I set out to help, or influence a community. None at all. No securities license in hand, no clients, and no proof of concept to give me the faith to act on what I believed would occur. Some will call it arrogance, others confidence, but what they think does not really matter for your building process.

It doesn't matter how far in the distant future it may seem, you need to be able to envision yourself in the seat in which you wish to sit. You have to see yourself in that time when cars can fly before you get there. If you cannot, you will be stuck between disbelief and action, which is where dreams go to die. The faster that you can envision yourself with the life that you are working to create, the faster the world will move aside to let you have it. This is what Coach Gould and the countless Master Wealth-Builders I have encountered in my professional life have shown me time after time.

◆ ◆ ◆

Mastering your mindset is the foundation for the following steps to creating long-term wealth. Shift your thoughts to shift your actions and make each of your long days count in getting you closer to your goals. If you do this, there will be no plan that you cannot follow and no situation that you cannot persevere through. You are built for this!

STEP 2

MASTER
THE PLAN

You can't build a reputation on what you're going to do.

– Henry Ford

3

The Four Financial Pitfalls—and How to Avoid Them

There are no accidents. There are no failures. There are only results. Every decision that we make yields an outcome.

Anybody who considers themselves financially secure has exhausted a plan to get them to that point. Like an Olympian, your process of manifesting the wealth illustrated in your dreams requires sacrifice, focus, and perseverance. That's why it's so important to start when you're young so you have the room to fail fast, to bounce back with energy and enthusiasm, and to make mastering wealth-building a lifelong practice.

But before you can master a plan, you have to develop one. Your financial plan is the compass that will guide you from your current condition to your future position. Most wealth management books first provide instructions on how to develop a plan, and then discuss the hurdles you may face along the way. In the spirit of counterintuitive thinking, I'm going to start with the four financial planning pitfalls. I guarantee that if you keep these in mind while you are developing and mastering your plan, you will stay on the right path to long-term wealth generation.

If you see your current self in the descriptions of any of these four pitfalls, do not be alarmed. That just means you are one of many, and by becoming aware of what is blocking your path you are taking the first step to removing it. Being objective in your assessment of yourself will give you the room and freedom to truly follow your plan.

Four Financial Pitfalls—and How to Avoid Them

1. "I don't have enough money."
2. Peer comparison.
3. "I'll do it myself."
4. Impatience.

Pitfall #1: "I don't have enough money"

"I don't have $250,000 to invest, so no one will want to work with me."

If you think you don't have enough money to begin planning for your goals, you'll never have enough money. In the investment industry, there is no designated asset number that makes you more or less qualified to begin financial planning. And luckily, the days of our grandparents' financial advisors (and their required minimums) are long gone. Thinking that you don't have enough money blocks you from getting the advice and direction you need to help you grow whatever you do have. And if you wait until the point where you feel like you have enough, you will have less time to implement the plan that you thought you needed $1 million to initiate.

Things are continually getting more expensive and more taxing on the Master Wealth-Builders who pursue their wildest dreams. Start now, while you have the time. Even a teenager with an after-school job can start mastering their plan by opening a Roth individual retirement account (more about these in chapter 5). The point is: No matter what you have or don't have, right now you have time. Use it. Master it. You won't regret it.

Pitfall #2: Peer comparison

In interviews with prospective clients, it blew my mind how many people knew (or thought they knew) the financial position of their peers. These comparisons inclined people to think that their assets were supposed to appreciate faster, that planning came second to risk-taking, and that they were "poor" although to me they were perfectly fine in financial terms.

A millionaire on a block full of billionaires will consider himself poor. But in reality, he's better off than almost everybody else in the country. Comparing yourself to your peers is the quicksand for the practice of *lifestyle inflation*, the tendency to spend more as you earn more. This costly habit has a domino effect that makes it extremely difficult for you to pay off debt and accumulate real assets. You begin to develop an affinity for acquiring things that you do not need and carry liabilities that will slow or stop your progress.

If you ever feel yourself comparing your own situation against your peers, stop and kick in the power of counterintuitive thinking. You will never truly understand how someone else reached their current financial status, and trying to make that comparison will only lead you to behaviors that are counterproductive to your plan. Comparison will influence you to make brash and often emotional decisions that could lead you away from your goals. Her story is not your story. His stocks are not yours.

Forget about the Joneses and how much money you think they have. Instead, foster a tunnel vision that focuses only on improving *your* financial status and inching you closer to *your* goals. Wherever you are, you are in a great spot to keep on moving along with your plan. You are the only one who can decide on your goals and the only one who can carry out your financial game plan. Keep your energy and focus in this productive place.

Pitfall #3: "I'll do it myself"

Let's have a brief slow clap for all those who can do it themselves. All two of you. All right! Now let's talk about what the rest of us can do.

When it comes to financial planning, there is a small group of people who can handle their financial plans from creation to implementation all by themselves. It's amazing. They're amazing. But what goes into doing it and doing it right is a lot of time. You're going to have to research investments, stick to a plan, and monitor everything diligently in order to make the correct moves so that you don't sell investments prematurely or make emotional decisions, and can harvest gains at an opportune time. These are all things you likely won't have the time to do consistently and with an objective eye. It is important to step outside of our egos, take with a grain of salt all the "water-cooler talk" about what everybody else at work is investing in, and seek help and accountability from a professional.

Pitfall #4: Impatience

Impatience makes wealth building impossible. Impatience leads you to change a sturdy plan multiple times to harvest small gains before they can grow into much larger ones. The lack of patience is like digging a seed from out of good soil before it sprouts. All plans take time, and most of your success when it comes to financial planning will be attributed to what you decide not to do rather than what you actually do.

Patience pays and the lack of it costs. It's that simple. When your perspective shifts to embrace this principle, your habits will as well. You have to starve your impatience and feed your discipline. This is where you have the advantage as a younger person. Whether you're a Gen Xer or a Millennial, you are many years away from the big retirement milestone, and perhaps still several years away from others. You have the time to practice the patience to stick to the plan.

Being young in this era means a number of things. You are encouraged to explore any and all possibilities. You are in a period of solstice in which you will likely experience the extremes of good and bad, and whatever happens you are young and vibrant enough to move along with hope for the future. Your creative juices are flowing and you have a knack for using and learning all of the new technology hitting the market. Unlike our parents and grandparents, you have access to all of the resources and information to build what you want, learn what you want, and manage life however you want.

Still, today's young professionals face unique challenges. The culture of the thirty-something-year-old in the modern era is much different than that of the young professional in the past. The technological age has conditioned growing adults to expect instant gratification for professional and personal goals alike. These expectations can breed a sense of entitlement and a lack of steadfastness that creates barriers to achieving every single goal that people make for themselves. Don't let that happen to you. This time provides the perfect opportunity to set the tone for the rest of your life and build great habits so later on down the line you won't have to spend your increasingly precious time breaking bad ones.

4

The Master Budget

When we talk about financial planning, it is the small battles that win the war. The biggest of these battles is the war within. So much can be learned about a person's priorities simply by watching what they spend their money on. The debit card has never told a lie, and your statements tell the tale of true Master Wealth-Building—or of wasted opportunities.

Take a look at your most recent month's bank statement. Better yet, the last two months—or three months if you are feeling really ambitious. If you skim your statements and think to yourself, "Man, I'm doing a good job," you are probably a conservative saver with the need to reallocate your hard-earned dollars to vehicles where they can work better for you (I'll get to that later). If your facial expression changes because you can smell the stench of your spending habits, well, that's a good thing too. You obviously recognize that some changes need to be made and that you have development opportunities within your current spending habits.

Your prudent day-to-day habits are what will inch you forward in your journey to long-term wealth generation. Quite frankly, sometimes budgeting in this manner sucks. It feels like you're making big sacrifices and is absolutely no fun—especially when your peers may be "making it rain" on unnecessary (but covetable) items and gadgets that they'll soon replace. I know, they are entirely bogus and incredibly tempting. Yet if you are experiencing these emotions of envy and restraint you might just be doing something right. It means you're sticking to your plan, reluctantly or otherwise.

Financial wellness consists of a long series of small victories won by executing your plan every day. Every day that you can stick to your plan is a day that you become closer to touching the wealth that you are working toward. Your ultimate victory lies in your ability to win the day. And so, before the stocks, mutual funds, and all the other sexy stuff that people like to talk about, you have to sit down with yourself and get to the nitty-gritty. The devil is in the details, and the details are in your Master Budget, a document that will act as your financial bible and serve as the set of procedures governing all of the inflows and outflows that you have on a monthly basis. I'll walk you through this.

Today, there are many mobile and web-based applications that people use for budgeting purposes. While these applications are great supplementary tools to make it easier to track your expenses, many are too impersonal to be used as your only budget tool. They prevent you from internalizing your budget and its unique constraints. How many push notifications do you ignore on a daily basis? One more push notification will not change your life, but one solid budget that you write down, continually revisit, and work every day toward mastering could change your financial life.

RIITE Planning Worksheet

Your Master Budget should be composed of everything that illustrates your financial life. Take a look at the RIITE (Retirement, Investments, Insurances, Taxes, and Estate Planning) worksheet we use for our clients at Berknell as an example (Figure 1). For simplicity, you can segment your Master Budget into five key parts: Income Information, Assets, Liabilities, Cash Flow, and Goals. Do you have your pen and paper ready? Good.

Income Information

On the first line, write *Income Information*. Here, as accurately as possible, list everything about all forms of income that you receive over the course of a given month. Start with your monthly gross income. Be sure to include any bonuses, rental income, and the dough you make from all of your side hustles. If the number is variable, list the worst-case scenario. Everything must be listed, because (dun, dun-dun!) soon come the taxes and deductions. Yes, it's true. The only thing guaranteed in life is death

Figure 1 RIITE Planning Worksheet

Personal Information

Name   _____
Date of birth   _____
Marital status _____
Children   _____

Employment and Income Information

Occupation   _____
Employer   _____
Annual income   _____
401(k) contribution rate   _____
Tax exemptions   _____
Dental   _____
Vision   _____
Medical insurance payments   _____
Health savings account (HSA)   _____
Flexible spending account (FSA)   _____

If applicable

Rental income   _____
HSA contributions   _____
Pretax medical benefit deduction _____
Pretax dental benefit deduction   _____
Pretax vision benefit deduction   _____
Pretax insurance deduction   _____

Retirement Accounts

Traditional IRAs _____
Roth IRAs   _____
401(k)   _____
Others   _____

Insurance

Life insurance (whole/term)   _____
Group (employee) life insurance   _____
Annuity contracts   _____

Investments

Individual accounts   _____
Joint accounts   _____
Trust accounts   _____
Education savings accounts   _____

Estate Plan

Circle Yes or No

Do you have a will?   Yes/No
Do you have a trust?   Yes/No
Have you designated beneficiaries on all your accounts? Yes/No

Assets

Checking account balance   _____
Savings account balance   _____
Home value   _____
401(k)/403(b) balance   _____
Certificates of deposit   _____
Trust fund balance   _____
Car value   _____
Boat value   _____

Liabilities

Car loan balance/interest rate   _____
                                       _____
                                       _____

Liabilities

Car loans/interest rates (*cont.*)   _____

_____

_____

Credit card balances/
interest rates   _____

_____

_____

_____

_____

_____

Home mortgage/
interest rates   _____

_____

Student loans/
interest rates   _____

_____

_____

_____

Cash Flow

Mortgage/rent   _____

Utilities   _____

Car loan/lease payment   _____

Life insurance premium   _____

Car insurance premium   _____

Car maintenance/fuel   _____

Food   _____

Entertainment   _____

Student loan payment   _____

Transportation   _____

Laundry/dry cleaning   _____

Emergency fund   _____

Other   _____

Goals

Rank your goals in order of priority from 1 to 7, with 1 being the highest:

Retirement planning   _____

Home purchase   _____

Education savings   _____

Cash flow management   _____

Investment management   _____

Debt reduction   _____

Insurance   _____

and taxes. It's not all bad, though. At least some of these deductions work in your favor.

This taxes and deductions portion may require some research on your behalf. Your paystubs will definitely come in handy. List every single deduction that comes out of your check before or after your net earnings. Every. Single. One. This will include but not be limited to federal and state taxes (if applicable), your retirement plan contribution, healthcare, dental and vision plan deductions, health savings account contributions, and Roth IRA and 401(k) contributions, among others. Now, calculate your net income number for the month. Take a deep breath. Don't panic. This is the number that you are working with to cover your monthly expenses.

If this number looks too small, you're probably already realizing that you need to shift from the Consumer mindset to the Master Wealth-Builder mindset. For most people, it takes very conscious and meticulous planning to stride toward your goals. Most of us aren't yet millionaires, and it often seems as if we need at least a couple of million dollars to get started. But don't be discouraged. Attack these speed bumps by planning fiercely. It will give you more hope to reach your financial goals.

Assets and Liabilities

Assets and Liabilities should also be listed in your Master Budget. Some people will argue against including them, but I believe it's important in giving you the full picture of your net worth and why you should save, pay down debt, and (most important) pay yourself first in the form of investments that grow your wealth over time. The very basic forms of your assets will be your checking and savings accounts, followed by your home value, retirement account balances (including traditional and Roth IRAs), employer-sponsored retirement accounts, certificates of deposit, and the value of any tangible assets like your car or a boat. Most of these assets are the cash and growth tools that will help you build your long-term wealth.

Now here come the *Liabilities*, the part that we never want to talk about. We all want to be owners and not loaners. Unfortunately, you cannot have one without giving up the lifestyle of the other. Let's face them head on. In this section should be everything that you owe to an entity or another person. You should include your car loan, the total balance of all of your credit cards, your home mortgage, and, of course, those student loans.

It is very important that both *Assets* and *Liabilities* are listed on your Master Budget because they will guide all the financial decisions that you make. I would argue that there are three reasons why people do not design their wealth in the ways that they could: lack of knowledge of their financial situation, lack of preciseness in their goals (see chapter 5), and lack of discipline. My point here is that if you have a strong idea of your strength and development opportunities, you'll be able to make sound day-to-day financial decisions.

The term "net worth" has been glamorized as something to flaunt among peers and admired by the general public. That's complete and utter malarkey. I'll use the word "malarkey." Net worth is something that billionaires and homeless people both have. It is literally the value of all your assets minus the value of your liabilities. Knowledge of your financial situation means knowing all of the components of your net worth, which means knowledge of every asset and liability on your Master Budget. If you have this information, at minimum, you will be conscious about your money decisions and the results that they yield. If you can be honest and clear with yourself, the odds of being more disciplined with your decisions rises dramatically.

Cash Flow

Let's talk a little bit more about discipline. Lack of discipline is a silent killer of the designs of Master Wealth-Builders. Our gross incomes listed in the *Income Information* segment are distractions that sway us into relaxation—which then shows up in our *Cash Flow*, the fourth component of the Master Budget. Traditionally, the cash flow statement is used to monitor a business's transactions over the course of a quarter. I believe that you should run your personal finances like a business with defined goals. I say this because a budget only acts as an allocation of the money you make, not a diagnosis of the mistakes that you are making. We see this all the time: people set parameters for how their money will be spent and things come up. Life happens. Allocations for spending alone are not enough. Yet allocations based on your plan comprise the "how" that gets you closer to your design for building wealth.

The *Cash Flow* section should list all of the things that you are spending your money on after taxes and deductions are taken out of your gross income—that is, your expenses. Under this section of your Master Budget, you should list all of your expenses, including your mortgage or rent payments, investment account contributions, auto loan payments, credit card payments, life insurance premiums, emergency funding, auto insurance, auto fuel and maintenance expenses, education loan payments, monthly food expenses, transportation expenses, dry cleaning, entertainment such as eating out and movies, and any other miscellaneous expenses that you might have. Overwhelmed yet? Good. Fill out each line with the exact or near exact amounts. Now draw a line and list the total below.

This figure alone can tell you a lot about your habits. You will be either at a deficit or a surplus. If you are at a deficit, this could mean that you are living above your means or your spending habits are unwise. You should take the time to look at areas where you can cut back on expenses (more on this coming up). If you are at a surplus, perhaps you are a strong budgeter, but have too much in savings and could be missing out on market returns. Regardless, this figure will give you a clear picture of your strengths and weaknesses and direct you to reallocating funds for your day-to-day activities more judiciously.

Goals

Napoleon Hill, the author of the timeless book *Think and Grow Rich*, says that you are what you say you are. I agree. The practice of speaking things into existence triggers neurochemicals that promote actions and behaviors. Your wealth design lies not only in the way that you think, but also in what you do. Most people can rank their goals out of eight choices: retirement, home purchase, education savings, cash flow management, investment management, debt reduction, insurance, and estate planning. How would you rank these eight goals for your life?

By prioritizing these goals and revisiting them on a set schedule, you'll be able to ingrain these priorities into your head. You will recommit over and over again to carrying out the actions that will bring you closer to achieving these goals. Listing your goals is the bow that ties the Master Budget together.

◆ ◆ ◆

You have to be your own budget police. Do your spending patterns align with your income? Does what you're spending your money on align with your listed goals and priorities? If not, how long has this mismatch been going on, and what opportunities have you missed as a result? Don't let it get to that place.

Your Master Budget is just words and numbers on paper if you do not follow it. For this reason, you should evaluate how your actions are aligning with your goals on an ongoing basis. By setting a routine schedule to assess your habits, you will be able to identify shortfalls quickly and recommit to and readjust your Master Budget.

Whether monthly or quarterly, set a time to update your net worth statement (your list of assets and liabilities) and evaluate your spending. These self-assessments should be milestone trackers to determine whether you are just talking the talk or actually walking the walk. The numbers don't lie, and I am confident that if you listen to what your Master Budget is telling you, your financial circumstance will change for the better—and fast.

The good part in all of this is that at this stage of your life, time is your friend. Go now and you'll go far.

5

Goal-Based Investing

The last component of the Master Budget is the prioritization of your goals. Why? Because once you prioritize your goals, your actions, as outlined in the *Cash Flow* section of your Master Budget, should follow.

Where your money is directed should mirror the goals that you have listed in your Master Budget in order of priority. As a goal is met, you can update your budget to move up whatever is next in line so that goal gets top priority and your top dollars. Sounds easy, doesn't it?

Different people will define investments in different ways. No matter how you cut it, an investment is a placement of your dollars that over time ends in a profit or material result. You should make money from your investments! Let no man or woman persuade you into thinking that that is not the case. The trajectory of how you make

that money will be based on risk tolerance for that investment. Still, the purpose of an investment is always for you
to win in the end.

The problem lies with the general public's narrow
perspective of what an investment is. Gains and profits,
though great when actual greenbacks land in your hand,
are not the only way someone can make money on an
investment or get closer to their goals. By assessing the
eight common goals of Master Wealth-Builders—retirement, home purchase, education savings, cash flow
management, investment management, debt reduction,
insurance, and estate planning—you can see that most
of Master Wealth-Building is not magic, but is instead
the product of math (and time). The only magic that is
involved lies in your consistency, resilience, and ability to
see yourself at the finish line while working like you're at
the starting line.

Home Purchase Goal

The purchase of a first home for many young professionals
is an "I've arrived" moment. This step signifies true adulthood, the payoff for hard work, and achievement of the
American Dream. But you should understand that there
are multiple moving parts that come into play when you
buy your first home, including qualification for a mortgage
loan, determining the amount you can put toward a down
payment, the potential need for property mortgage insurance, and tax liabilities. This is just the short list before you
even take a look at your potential house! When we get to
the math, you'll see that how you've been saving may or

may not be the best way to go about the purchase of your first home.

First things first: Your savings account alone won't do it. In fact, your savings account could be detrimental to your home purchase goal, simply based on a little principle called *inflation*. For the last three decades, America has experienced falls in interest rates to historic lows. This means that the same savings account you have now—the one that pays you the half of a percent that you're so excited about—used to pay upwards of 3 percent. Meanwhile, the costs of goods and services are continuing to increase over time, with inflation running at about a 3 percent increase annually. What this means is that your savings account that is "earning" you 0.5 percent annually is actually *losing* you 2.5 percent by not keeping up with or exceeding the 3 percent inflation rate that raises the cost of the things you enjoy year after year. Yeah, you're robbing yourself!

So what do I do, you ask? You begin with clear details about the home of your dreams: its price, your down payment, and when you want to buy it. After you figure this out, it's nothing but math. You'll need three or four critical components to do the calculations for yourself: how much you have, a realistic expectation of how much you'll make from investing, a time horizon or deadline for your home purchase, and how much you will contribute on a defined schedule to this goal. With this information, you'll be able to calculate how much of a down payment you can afford and change the number of years or rate of return based on the probability of this happening. The only "magic" needed is your ability to invest with a detailed long-term goal in mind. (For more on mastering real estate, go to chapter 6.)

Cash-Flow Management Goals

If budgeting and goals-based investing were sports, your cash-flow statement would be your film study. Most athletes monitor their performance and correct their flaws by watching themselves on film. Here they can see all the minute details of the movements that they need to improve to get closer to their goals. In the same way, studying your cash flow will show you all the minute details of how to improve your spending to bring you closer to your financial goals. There's no magic bullet to meeting cash-flow management goals. It's clear and simple: You have a responsibility to cut or reallocate your expenses in order to be cash-flow positive and to meet your goals in the order that you have prioritized them. This is on you, and if your cash-flow statement doesn't reflect those priorities, periodic evaluation of your Master Budget will continue to sound the alarm.

Positive cash flow is not about how much money you make. Whether you think you make a lot or a little, being a good steward of your money is the key to living well and being able to handle more of it. Look at your life and ask yourself what goods or services you are paying for that you can make or do for yourself or get for free. Saving money in a few small areas can lead to big rewards. Here are a few examples of how to cut back:

Live with your parents. One of the biggest expenses for a Master Wealth-Builder in his roaring twenties stems from his desire to be fully independent. Living on your own, paying your own bills, and having the freedom to do what you want are the hallmarks of adulthood. But according to a study by the Pew Research Center, more than 36 percent of Millennials from ages eighteen to thirty-six live at home with their parents. Although a number of factors often force young adults to live at home, there are many reasons that staying at home may be a good option. The biggest one is the amount of cash you can save versus renting an apartment.

Rent cheap. Of course, not everyone has the luxury of living at home. If you must rent, rent cheap. Renting can be a good solution if you work far away from your parents' home or need a place to live temporarily—and the best way to rent is with an end in mind. The rule of thumb is that your housing costs should be—at most—28 percent of your gross income. If you are renting, try to come under this 28 percent suggested rate if you can. You can also consider renting a room or getting a roommate to reduce your costs. By renting cheap, you can still save money, leaving room for other wealth-generation activities like transitioning into owning a property.

Skip happy hour. Being social plays a big role in our lives—but the cost of all those happy hours can quickly add up. Instead of going to happy hour to eat and drink, go strictly to socialize with colleagues and friends. If social drinking is very important to you, then make sure to cap your expenses in your Master Budget.

Make your own dinner. Eating out may be one of the biggest dampers in your Master Wealth-Building efforts. Unlike renting, which is circumstantial and necessary for some, eating out can be completely avoided. I'm not saying you should never eat out. Having a life is important, plus you've worked hard for your money. I just want you to consider that the money spent on meals out could also be spent on income-generating investments that will be worth much more years later than that fancy dinner is worth now. If eating out is an important social activity for you, think about inviting friends over for a fun night in.

Drive efficiently. There are many options for you to get from point A to point B that do not involve a monthly car payment. I have not owned a car for nearly three years, and I do not regret it at all. To me, a car is just another bill that takes up space on my Master Budget. By using car-share services and myriad public transportation options, my commutes have been faster and more cost-efficient. If your family circumstances require that you have a car to get to work or get your kids to school, a fuel-efficient or electric car may be the best investment. Year over year, you'll save money on oil and gas costs, which means more income and lower outflows.

Shop for car insurance. Instead of going with a name-brand insurance carrier or the first option you run across, be sure to shop around and find a company that suits your needs within your budget for car insurance.

Make your own coffee. I love to have my coffee in the morning, and you probably do too. But grande lattes at retail prices are ridiculously marked up! If you must have a cup of joe, home-brew your coffee for pennies on the dollar compared to your favorite coffee house.

Find the deal. When financial professionals write about saving, it can easily take the fun out of life. The objective is not to make life boring, but to make life possible. By finding good deals on trips for hotels and airfare, you can enjoy the luxuries of life at a lower cost. Consider traveling during off-peak seasons when fares and other costs are much lower than during busy times.

Ditch the landline. You're probably thinking, "Who uses landlines anymore?" and for good reason. Landlines can be useful in the event of emergencies, but your cell phone is just as effective. According to the US Bureau of Labor and Statistics in its 2015 study, American families are spending $353 a year for landlines in addition to the $963 that they spend on cell phones. The story of the landline is the story of the evolution of technology. If you can live without it, cut it off and save that money!

Get rid of cable. Your monthly cable bill is an extremely big spend. When assessing my clients' Master Budgets, it intrigues me how much individuals pay for cable that, outside of big games and a few shows, they do not watch at all. Many people shell out $100 to $250 per month to watch television only occasionally. If you need some form of visual entertainment, streaming sites and services like HBOGo, FireStick, Netflix, and Hulu will allow you to watch movies, documentaries, and television series for a fraction of the price.

Wear a sweater. As a child, I did not dare mention to my mom that we should turn on the heater. We did not have the extra money, for starters. Second, she wanted to "fix" the utility costs. Utility bills become variable expenses when you are unable to "fix" them. Heat and air-conditioning expenses can put a dent in your pocketbook in the winter and summer, especially when you do not monitor their use. Be sure to keep tabs on the use of your heating and air conditioning. If you can keep these costs within a small range, you'll save yourself from surprises every month.

Ditch the gym. As a former athlete, I'm a big advocate for living a healthy, active lifestyle—and there are an abundance of ways to live healthy without a monthly gym membership. If you do not use your membership as frequently as it would take to justify the cost, it may be time to ditch the gym. If you have access to a gym in your residence, or are able to do a home workout or cardio exercise around your neighborhood, you can stack dollars to invest in more worthy wealth-building efforts.

Make a grocery list. Writing a fictitious number under groceries on your Master Budget does not mean that you are going to stick to spending that amount. Successful master planning means mastering the details. Food is a necessity, but many people find themselves buying things they do not need while in the grocery store. Be sure to check your inventory before going grocery shopping and list the things that you need so that you can stay within the budget defined on your sheet. Monitor deals and use coupons to take advantage of additional savings.

Don't follow the hype. We are professionals at confusing things that we want with things that we need. A plethora of cool gadgets and technologies are released by the world's most popular companies every day, and it may seem that everyone has them. Focus on your own needs and reserve a small space for wants. If you do this, you'll always have the right tools to build.

Look for opportunities. There will always be opportunities to earn, which means opportunities to save. Your job is to make sure that you're aware of these opportunities and are not subjecting yourself to lifestyle inflation, the process of adding expenses as your income increases. The opportunities you can find to save money will generate opportunities to make your money work for you. Who wants to work forever because they have to? What brings you closer to the lifestyle you want and the prosperity you deserve will be your ability to realize the myriad small opportunities to save and invest. If you are able to do so early and often, you'll get to your destination much quicker.

A word on emergency funds. If you don't already have an emergency fund, regular monthly contributions to one should definitely be a line item in your cash-flow statement. People who do not take this step often get in the way of their own progress. Investments fluctuate and life happens; without a fund earmarked for unexpected costs you may be forced to reverse the course of the compound interest by taking withdrawals from an investment account. You will lose out on all the time you previously put into growing that money.

The emergency fund rules are the same everywhere: Save three to six months of your expenses in a risk-adverse, insured, liquid account. The vague part about this rule is what determines saving three months versus saving six months of your income. Here's how I break it down: If you are a full-time single earner, lean on the side closer to three months. If you are single and working a part-time job with no assistance from parents or a significant other, you should prepare for six months. If you are married and both of you are employed, the emergency fund should be closer to three months of monthly expenses. If only one person in a couple is working, with no access to an inheritance or assistance from family, their goal should be six months of expenses saved in an emergency account. As you get older, accumulate more familial responsibilities, and acquire more assets, your emergency fund requirements should continue to increase. You will have to calculate how much you need in your fund based on your expenses and income and evaluate your access to other resources to have that amount available to you in the event of an emergency.

Last point: Your emergency fund should be housed in an FDIC-insured, low-volatility account that is liquid and relatively easy to access. Money market accounts and traditional savings account are two of the best alternatives for holding your emergency fund and are easy to set up.

Debt Reduction Goals

In addition to your employer-sponsored accounts, many personal finance books recommend that you invest in the stock market, real estate, and other opportunities. They tell you to head straight to the market if you want to grow your wealth and park your money there over the long term, and they suggest (they don't quite promise) that down the line you'll be rich! In many ways, this is true. Investing requires patience and consistency over a long period of time. But what's also true is that most Americans do not have the cash flow to do any of those things, largely because their money is tied up in debt. You can't start to build wealth if the money that you would use to do so is parked on your credit card balances and increasing as interest adds up. The way that I see it, high-interest debt is silently robbing us—and we're letting it! It's a trap. The best financial return that we will ever get on our money will be paying off the balances of our high-interest-rate debt.

Debt reduction might be the number one goal for most Americans. Even though we have a lot of information available to us on the topic of debt, we are still a very debt-heavy people. The numbers do not lie. According to Nerdwallet, Americans are neck-deep in debt, and not only due to lifestyle inflation. Things are just too expensive, from food to rent to healthcare, and our paychecks aren't catching up. The average household has credit card debt of $16,425, and additional debt in the form of car loans, mortgages, and student loans totaling over $135,000. If you are a young person starting out or in the middle of your professional career, you probably know firsthand what these debt statistics mean and what that debt load feels like.

The pro side of this is that if you start early, you'll be able to quickly knock out this debt and have plenty of time left to save and invest in things that will grow your money. The con is if you're like most other people, you don't even know where to start. In truth, there is no real secret to paying down debt. Most people exercise one of the two most common strategies: snowballing debt payments and paying more than the minimum.

Snowballing debt payments. This is a time-tested strategy that allows individuals with many outstanding balances to pay them simultaneously in a way that earns many small wins that yield big results. There are several ways that you can go about implementing this method. Since you've already done yourself the favor of listing all of your liabilities in your Master Budget, you'll be able to look at your debt, specifically your credit cards, and assess the balance amounts and interest rates on those balances.

One way to initiate the snowball method is the balance transfer strategy. Take a long, hard look at the interest rates on all of your credit cards. There is a huge chance that the interest rates vary among your credit cards. Now reach out to the credit card provider with the lowest interest rate and ask if you are eligible for a balance transfer. If you are eligible, transfer the balance from your high-interest card to your low-interest card and then begin your routine payments. The drop in your interest rate can lead to hundreds of dollars saved.

A second approach comes into play if your balances are too big to transfer all to a single card. In this case, pay the minimum balances on all your cards except for the one with the smallest balance. Pay that one off more aggressively, hopefully with dollars that you saved from cutting out unnecessary expenses from the *Cash Flow* section of your Master Budget. Notch your first win by paying that card off completely, and then repeat the process with the remaining cards and the next largest balance.

Paying more than the minimum. A credit card balance of $2,000 at a 20 percent annual interest rate costs you $400 per year in interest if you're just paying the minimum required each month. Money spent on interest is money lost. Gone. That $400 that you lost can work for you through an investment, but first your debt needs to be paid off.

Minimum payments are a mechanism to extend payments to creditors that works to convince you that you're being responsible—while they squeeze out interest from your pocketbook for as long as possible. By paying only the minimum amount required, you are giving the creditor the advantage. But if you pay more than the minimum required each month in order to get rid of credit card debt as soon as possible, the money you save on interest becomes your rate of return. Every payment made on a high-interest credit card is a return that would be extremely difficult for you to make with average stock market performance. For example, in average market conditions, it would take multiple years for you to earn 20 percent through the investments that you hold in your accounts.

Bottom line: If you have debt, your highest-priority goal should be reducing it.

Retirement and Investment Management Goals

You're probably asking yourself, "What is the difference between retirement and investment management goals?" That's a good question. In retirement, you won't have income from employment because, duh, you'll be retired. Strategizing for your retirement requires that you know exactly what you want to do in retirement and how you'd like to live. You'll need to calculate "your number," that is, an amount that you'd like to save from now until the year that you plan to retire. You'll need to know how much your retired self will be spending on a yearly basis, your tax bracket, and how much additional assistance you'll get from the government, such as through Social Security and Medicare. Trying to figure all this out now might give you a brain freeze. But say it with me again: It's not magic, it's math. Like many others, I did not really like math (and sometimes still do not) until I figured out that understanding numbers could have a dramatic effect on my goals.

The quickest way to begin to plan for retirement is to put money away in addition to your employer-sponsored retirement account. Open a Roth or traditional IRA, then begin systematically investing. *Dollar cost averaging* is a systematic, risk-mitigating investment strategy that requires the investor to choose a frequency for investing a stated amount of money. For example, you commit to making a $100 contribution to your investment account on the fifteenth of every month. This is beneficial because it is not contingent upon timing or the state of the market, which often complicates the process. It also allows you to account for the payment in your Master Budget. Platforms like Betterment and Wealthfront have made it easy for Millennials and Gen Xers to get started on their IRAs without worrying about account minimums and wolfish financial advisors.

Investment management, to me, is reserved for the goals that are in between where you are and where you want to be in retirement. It could be savings for your child's education, buying your first or second home, or saving up for a wedding. Regardless, you'll have to have your numbers in order so that a trusted professional can tell you if your expectations are too lofty given the amount of money that you are working with. This is goal-based investing in its truest form, and the gains will show in the traditional manner of percentage increases. (For more on mastering investing, go to chapter 7.)

Insurance Goals

The top four ways to become rich are an inheritance, marrying wealthy, winning the lotto, and entrepreneurship. While I believe wealth consists of more than money, it is no secret that money can change the way that future wealth is built; it can increase options and opportunities and influence the ways that the next generation of Master

Wealth-Builders can build upon your design. There are few things that are surer than life insurance to help your heirs continue to run the Master Wealth-Building race that you began. Whether you are starting from a firm foundation or from scratch, insurance can be a way to guarantee that whoever is following you does not start from the same place that you had to.

The two most popular types of life insurance policies are term and whole life insurance. Term insurance insures a person for a designated period of time. For example, if you purchase a thirty-year term life insurance policy at age thirty, you will be insured until age sixty. Term life policies are cheaper than whole life policies and can be much easier to understand. Unlike a term life policy, a whole life policy is permanent. These policies do not expire and cost much more than term life insurance policies. The insurance agent's selling point is the tax-sheltered savings mechanism, called cash value, that whole life policies offer. While the policy can pay interest (usually at a very low rate), its cost often does not justify the value of the interest to be paid to the holder. Yet agents sell these products as a "win-win." The phrase "win-win" has always been my sign to run. If those words are uttered, I'll meet you at the exit. Another thing to note: Policies can lapse if scheduled payments are not made on time, making it important for you to consider what you can afford before choosing such a policy.

The best advice for life insurance is to shop around for policies that cover your needs and fit within your price range. At a minimum, buy term life insurance and invest the difference.

Estate Management Goals

Estate planning can be a complex ordeal. Usually it requires an attorney and lots of paperwork, and it could cost you a pretty penny. Thinking about your death is something that not many young people want to do. I bet estate planning is one of the last priorities in your Master Budget. My advice is to designate beneficiaries for all of your accounts. This way, in the event of the unthinkable, your assets will avoid the probate process and will go directly to your designated beneficiaries. If you have a family, however, consider taking it further and consulting an attorney for a will and estate plan.

◆ ◆ ◆

If you can sit through the rough times and be disciplined through the good times, you will increase your likelihood of building the wealth you desire early on. Because, let's face it, the catch-up game is hard. Catching up on debt payments, retirement planning, and emergency fund savings can be done, but it's difficult. If you start now, you will save yourself from the exhausting task of having to catch up at a later date.

Procrastination only stifles and deadens your efforts. Being young gives you one chance to avoid that painful process of catching up because you took the time to get ahead. Follow your Master Budget and the goals that you prioritized for yourself and you'll live a life that most cannot because you took the time to do what they would not.

Step 3

MASTER YOUR INCOME

You'll never reach your destination if you stop and throw stones at every dog that barks.

–Winston Churchill

6

Until You Get Punched in the Face

One of the greatest boxing matches of our time was the Mike Tyson versus Evander Holyfield bout in Las Vegas, Nevada, in 1996. For months, sports journalists from near and far followed both fighters leading up to fight night for what was promised to be an extraordinary display of physical ability, speed, agility, and passion. The fight was marketed as a night that the world would remember.

Evander Holyfield came off as the calmer fighter of the two. As the camera documented him during sneak peeks of his training process, he had little to say and he meant business. He was six feet tall and weighed in at 226 pounds. His style was powerful and intimidating, and he wanted nothing more than to prove that he deserved his crown as the heavyweight champion of the world. For Holyfield, this was more than just a boxing match.

It was a long-awaited competition between two of the best fighters in the world that had been six years in the making.

Tyson had a similar stature and was a fierce and powerful competitor whose quickness and speed overwhelmed opponents and whose fights often ended early. He was as well a media professional's fondest dream. Often, during prefight coverage, journalists would fish for quotes and bring up Tyson's past, easily angering the fighter and provoking him to provide front-page material for the world to feast on. Tyson experienced a series of mishaps with bad publicity, including a devastating loss at the hands of Buster Douglas, and was eager to get his career back on track and reclaim his throne. The stage was set for the comeback of all time.

The official weigh-in and press conference at the MGM Grand Garden Arena drew in news reporters and fans from around the world. The tension that night was palpable and the energy pulsating. If looks could kill, both fighters would have been dead. The world could not wait and neither could the competitors.

The most memorable moment during the prefight festivities was in an interview with Tyson. Reporters sidled up to Tyson to get a quotable line and to assess the mood of the fighter. They prodded Tyson by complimenting Evander's fighting style: *He's strong. He's agile. He has superior lateral movement. He's one of the most powerful fighters since Muhammad Ali. How will you react to his game plan? How do you plan on beating him when you could not even beat Buster Douglas?*

As the questions continued, a frustrated Tyson stopped, looked one reporter in the eyes, and replied, "Everyone has a plan, until they punched in the face." This single quote is something that I have carried with me for a long time.

Life has definitely punched me in the face, and I'm sure it has bloodied your lip as well. We all know that great things do not happen by chance. It takes a lot of grit, planning, execution, and perseverance to take a goal from mindset to manifestation. Mastering your wealth is not about following a rigid step-by-step protocol that will get you to your goal. It is not about following the exact footsteps of someone who has already achieved the wealth that you desire. It is not even about making the best stock picks when investing. Mastering your wealth, above all else, depends on how you handle adversity when you get hit.

On November 8, Tyson's response to the many journalists was his way of saying that life happens. There was absolutely no way that he could predict what would happen during his fight with Evander Holyfield. Would he get punched in the mouth? Certainly. Yet there were times that Holyfield would get hit as well. As a fighter his only job was to make sure that he was prepared. As a Master Wealth-Builder, your job is to make sure that you are prepared as well.

Bracing Your Structure

When you're young, it's easy to think you are invincible, that you can withstand anything that life throws at you, that nothing can bring you down. True, your youth gives you much more time to recover from tragedy—and the strength and vitality to pick yourself up—but no one (and no plan) is really safe from one of life's knockout punches. The most you can do is find the best ways to brace yourself for whatever may come your way.

Take San Francisco. The City by the Bay straddles one of the most active fault lines on the West Coast. That means that residents like myself live under the constant threat of an earthquake. I remember the many mandatory earthquake drills I participated in as an elementary school student. At the sound of the fire alarm, we were prompted to take cover underneath our desks to practice how we would shield ourselves from falling objects in the event of an earthquake. The lights would flicker and sirens would sound as we waited for our teachers to line us up to proceed to the designated area where we would gather with the rest of the student body.

As students from kindergarten to fifth grade piled into a parking lot surrounded by tall buildings, I thought about what would happen if the buildings were damaged or collapsed. Being a curious kid, I asked my teacher, Mr. Chow, who explained that they equip the buildings with cross braces to ensure they stay up.

Cross braces are architectural systems that support buildings like my elementary school in the event of an earthquake. The X-shaped design ensures that in the event of a natural disaster the building has additional reinforcement to hold it up. Its sole purpose is to keep the building standing. Much like installing cross braces on the many retrofitted buildings in San Francisco, mastering your income will brace and support your wealth-generation plan, making it tougher to demolish in the face of life's natural and inevitable pressures.

Mastering income means freedom from financial stress, more options, and more opportunities. It allows your income, ideally from multiple sources, to act as a support for your current and future plans. It is important to note that while earnings from employment is a big piece of the Income Pie, the world of income stretches far beyond what is written on an offer letter or what you gross year after year.

There are unlimited ways to master income and there really is no ceiling for the amount of money that you can make. This infinite possibility can be a gift and a curse. The number of options for income can be overwhelming and, as Winston Churchill said, "You'll never get to your destination by throwing a stone at every dog that barks." That means you will have to say no to some things and you will have to say yes to the right things. In this section, I give you the tools to determine what are the right choices for you and your plan.

There are three time-tested ways to master income: the stock market, entrepreneurship, and real estate. No matter which strategy you choose (and maybe you'll decide to work them all!), remember that when you choose to pursue a dream, you have to prepare to deal with the risks that may be involved. The rest of this chapter explores how you can leverage real estate and your own entrepreneurship to master income. The next chapter focuses on how you can master the stock market, one of the most powerful (and intimidating) wealth-building vehicles out there.

Mastering Entrepreneurship

There is a unique group of leaders who not only seek to correct or improve the path that they walk, but to solve problems for themselves and others. They dedicate their lives to creating better technology, goods, services, and opportunities for themselves and the world around them by acting on their ideas. We call these people entrepreneurs.

Entrepreneurship is glorified in our society. Those who find success by challenging the status quo are exalted, praised, and admired. In fact, entrepreneurship is no different from the wealth-building process in which we are all already engaged. An entrepreneur must master thought to determine how an idea can not only solve a problem but also generate revenue. She must design and master a plan to take the idea to fruition, which takes sacrifice, commitment, and big-picture thinking. She must understand how to make her income work for her to support the execution of her idea, while controlling for the inevitable money drains and unforeseen circumstances that stand in the way of her plan's success.

Not all Master Wealth-Builders are entrepreneurs, but we all have the tools to be entrepreneurial: problem-solving, providing a service, and disrupting the norm. In addition, at this stage of your life you have less to lose by going full-throttle after your ideas than you will down the line. Take advantage!

So, you want to build wealth through entrepreneurship? Here's what you do:

1. **Solve a Problem.** Some of the world's biggest companies started with solving a small problem. Fixing a small problem was the starting point for Joe and Brian, who were having trouble paying their rent in San Francisco. It didn't take much to see that many people in one of the country's most expensive cities had the same problem. From this small idea, the pair set up three mattresses in their apartment and rented them out to people in need of temporary housing. Next came the website, and then the patrons, and with trial and error, a company was born. Airbnb is now one of the world's largest booking sites and houses millions of people every year. Joe and Brian's intent may not have been to change the world, but in solving their own problem they have changed the way that we look at the hotel industry and have mastered their own incomes (an understatement) in the process.

2. **Provide a Service.** Anyone can create and sell a service. If you have a trade or unique expertise, you can leverage your skills to provide more income for yourself and your family. The gig economy is a relatively low-risk way to dip your toes into the pool of service entrepreneurship and generate extra income. Companies like Lyft, Uber, Fiverr, and Task Rabbit have made it easy to provide services that fit our skill sets and resources and that can be easily incorporated into our schedules. The

other plus is that you get to work as a contractor on your own terms without the demands of or supervision from a hierarchy of managers.

While the gig economy can be enticing, there are, of course, downsides. Most important, you must understand the time/reward trade-off before you dive in. These are gigs. They are meant to be short projects that generate, in many cases, small amounts of cash per transaction. Be sure to allocate a designated amount of time for contracting per week as if it were a salaried job. And be aware of the volume of transactions necessary with any particular gig in order to reach your goals and the amount of time it will take for you to do so.

3. **Disrupt the Norm.** In the wake of a series of fatal race-related shootings by authorities, Morgan DeBaun took issue with the way that such news was being delivered by the mainstream media. She left her high-paying Silicon Valley job to build Blavity, a media platform that gives millions of Millennials the freedom to write, share, and discuss the issues they deem important and that other news outlets may miss. Morgan is one in an endless list of entrepreneurs who have created a new normal. She is an example of what using your talents can look like. You are talented, you are magnificent, and you are capable of building anything that you put your mind to. Like the plan that you are working on, you just have to start.

Master Real Estate

It is no secret why over 75 percent of millionaires have real estate in their portfolios: It makes them money! For many Baby Boomers, real estate has been the key to mastering income. But for their children and for the victims of the latest financial crisis, real estate is something they would warn investors to approach with caution.

Real estate is an asset that, in many cases, carries the attributes of a liability. An asset is something that pays you. A liability is something that you owe versus something that you own. In recent years, the debate on whether real estate is an asset or a liability has grown louder and louder. Most people are not shelling out hundreds of thousands of dollars at one time to purchase a home or property in full. The process usually requires an amount to be paid over a period of time, which gives a real estate "asset" the characteristics of a "liability." In addition, a real estate purchase can come with liabilities outside of the loan itself, such as insurance, property taxes, repairs, and maintenance. Even if you have fully paid off your mortgage, tax liens can still get your property snatched from right under you.

With a real estate investment, your job is to convert your property into a *functional asset*. A functional asset puts money in your pocket, minimizes your expenses, and can provide cash flow. Where real estate fits into your plan depends on how you want the asset to function—for example, as near-term extra income or as a financial stepping stone for the next generation of your family.

There are four ways to incorporate real estate into your wealth-building plan:

4. **Home Purchase.** The function of real estate for someone who is simply seeking to create a foundation for
their wealth-building plan is appreciation. For those
of us who have never known wealth in dollar terms, a
home purchase will be one of the first major tangible
contributions to our plan. There are two ways you can
hope to see your home increase in value: market appreciation and forced appreciation. Market appreciation
is great for the long-term wealth-builder. While not
generating hard cash, a home purchase is something
that through market growth and the paying down of
debt means more equity ownership for you. Forced
appreciation is the intentional uptick of value due to
renovations and additions to the property made by
the owner. This type of appreciation requires cash and
home improvements that can be extremely expensive. If you have the cash on hand and intend to sell
the home by a defined date, this could be a great way
to build home equity and use the proceeds from the
sale to reinvest in other areas (see more on investment
properties below).

5. **Rental Properties.** Rental properties are a fantastic
idea if you have the funds and understand the pros and
cons of managing them. In terms of mastering income,
owning a rental property means that you're the boss.
You choose who rents the space, what the space will
look like, how much the rent will be, and how you will
manage the operation. But you must consider exactly
how much you will earn after paying for principal,

interest, taxes, and insurance (PITI), and contributing a portion of the net income, typically 10 percent, as a sinking fund for maintenance costs, vacancy coverage, and upkeep. Here's how it breaks down: You're a property owner renting out your four-unit apartment complex to four tenants. The mortgage on the property is $3,200 per month, or $800 per unit. You decide to rent each unit out for $1,200 apiece. You think, "Every month I'll make $400 per unit. Perfect!" That's $1,600 per month that you'd make after paying PITI on the property. Now, let's contribute 10 percent into your sinking fund for vacancies and repairs: $160 per month. Your earnings are now $1,440 per month. But your property also has homeowner's association fees and property management fees, so now you add on an additional 15 percent in costs. Your net income is now $1,200—nothing to scoff at, but not the $1,600 you were initially hoping for.

6. **Investment Properties.** House flipping is a growing trend in the real estate market. Investors acquire properties that need to be improved, then after making the renovations sell them for a higher price, typically within the first twelve months of the purchase. However, the investor is responsible for the mortgage and associated costs until she makes the sale, which makes flipping a risky deal. The growing popularity of real estate shows on TV has given viewers the impression that anyone can flip properties, but this practice should only be reserved for those who have adequate resources. For

those who do, high rates of return can be realized quicker than with other investment options, and the tangible nature of the asset can offer a high degree of peace of mind.

7. **Real Estate Investment Trusts (REITs).** Real estate investment trusts are a great alternative for those who are not ready to purchase a home or use an income property for cash flow. Equity REITs are exchange-traded securities that invest in real estate and real estate operations. They are professionally managed and earn income via leases from tenants. The function of a REIT in your portfolio is to provide passive income, since they offer above-average dividends. By law, a real estate investment trust must distribute a staggering 90 percent of its taxable earnings to its shareholders in the form of dividends. That requirement means that you'll receive a portion of the billion-dollar operations earnings on a frequent basis.

Real estate can be tricky, and the purchase of such a huge asset should be discussed with qualified profession-als. On the other hand, becoming an entrepreneur takes a certain type of ambition and a high risk tolerance. Maybe you're not feeling ready to master your income in these ways just yet. So, let's talk about my favorite topic: the stock market.

While the stock market can carry just as much risk as any of the other ways to master income, it is vital to your success as a Master Wealth-Builder and can be a great way to put your money—however much you have or don't have—to work. Without it, you're looking at a house built on sand. With it, you're designing a house built on concrete. I'd choose the latter.

7

Mastering the Stock Market

The stock market is integrated into every facet of our lives. When a major event happens, media outlets are on it immediately with analysis on how the event will affect the market. Our employee-sponsored retirement accounts are tied to the stock market. Our phones have applications and widgets that track market performance on a daily basis and allow investors to trade securities at the click of a button. It is an extremely accessible way to multiply your hard-earned dollars and harvest income at retirement.

The stock market can be a key tool if you use it properly—but it's a dangerous tool if mishandled. Your success at mastering income via the stock market depends on how you'd like to grow your assets, how you diversify them, the amount of risk you agree to assume, the actual investments that you choose, and the returns you're able to gen-erate—particularly over the long term. It does no good for you to hit one home run and then strike out in every investment after that. That's just as bad as starting back at square one every year. It is my hope that the investing concepts outlined in this chapter will help you to lever-age the stock market as a cross brace for your long-term wealth-building plan.

Why Not Every Idea Is a Good One

Not every "hot" investment idea will align with what you seek to build. What is a good fit for you in your twenties may not be the best investment for you in your forties. In addition, the risk that you are personally willing to take may not be the same as another person would take on in the same situation. Investments must also align with your nonfinancial priorities. For example, if you are a socially conscious investor you will want to assess the environ-mental impact of a company before you make an invest-ment in it.

An investment must be analyzed to assess how it fits into what you want for decades to come—not just in the short term. You are investing for the day that cars fly, remember? Your investment decisions deserve much more thought than a quick recommendation from a coworker or a headline touting the latest initial public offering. Fur-thermore, your holding period for investments should be forever—or at least until the company that you choose experiences a fundamental change and no longer serves the purpose in your portfolio that it once did. If you take this approach, holding on to your investments regardless of whether the stock market is depressed or roaring will be much easier to do.

To help you with finding the right investments for you and your circumstances, you should create an *Investment Policy Statement*. Like the Master Budget for your daily expenses, the Investment Policy Statement will be the roadmap for how you will invest and what things you will look for in an investment. Without such a planning overview, you'll be vulnerable to making emotional decisions and abandoning your investment strategy at the first sign of market volatility.

Start with Asset Allocation

Asset allocation is the percentage breakdown by asset type that a Master Wealth-Builder holds in her investment portfolio. It is one of the first things to consider when making your investment policy statement. Whether it is 90 percent stocks and 10 percent bonds that an investor holds or an entire cash portfolio (which I'd never recommend), the asset allocation should be clearly outlined for a number of reasons:

1. **Understanding and Managing Your Risks.** Your asset allocation provides an overview of the risk level you are assuming. There is an inherent risk with however you structure your portfolio, even if you have taken what is considered to be a very conservative position. For example, allocations weighted heavier to stocks tend to be a lot more volatile than allocations with more bond

holdings. We can summarize this concept as "more risk, more reward" to help you manage your expectations for your portfolio: You cannot expect Ferrari returns with minivan risk. Your task is to choose an allocation that aligns with your risk and growth preferences.

2. **Investment Selection.** Your preferred allocation determines the type of assets you choose and how much you invest in each. For example, if you have an asset allocation weighted 90 percent to stocks and 10 percent to bonds, with a $100,000 portfolio balance you'd appropriately allocate $90,000 to equities and $10,000 to bonds and more conservative investments.

3. **Rebalancing.** This is a fancy word for getting an investor's portfolio back to the stated allocation in the event of growth or loss. For example, if your 90 percent stock/10 percent bonds portfolio loses value to become 80 percent stocks/20 percent bonds, your goal should be to rebalance the portfolio to get it back to a 90/10 allocation. You could do this by selling 10 percent of your bond allocation and then using those proceeds to purchase enough stock to bring you back to your chosen 90 percent stock allocation. This is the fundamental investment practice of *buying low and selling high*. Without a designated asset allocation, Master Builders are prone to making poor decisions that can be counterproductive to their goals (such as buying more bonds because your stock value went down).

4. **Ignoring the Herd.** The herd mentality is a well-known phenomenon in the investment industry. This instinct speaks to an investor's failure to make decisions for himself based on an assessment of his own best interests and his willingness to follow whatever is the popular idea at the time. Investing with the near term in mind and in faddish companies only leaves the design vulnerable to collapse. By committing to an asset allocation that is in line with your risk and growth profiles, you avoid the herd mentality and ensure that you are making investment decisions that serve your long-term goals.

Mastering Your Portfolio

"Never put all your eggs in one basket."

"Diversify your assets."

"You should have seven streams of income."

"Your portfolio is only as good as it is diversified."

Popular culture has developed mantras for simplifying the meaning of diversification that stretch most people too far and too thin when it comes to their investments. The word "diversification" leads us to think that we should spread our dollars across a large pool of investments. But this practice is foolish because, as I explained earlier, not every investment is fit for every person. Diversification should mean concentrating your efforts on high-quality, cost-effective investments that each has a defined purpose in your portfolio. Focusing on quality and not quantity minimizes the number of holdings you have but can maximize your portfolio's performance. Using this approach, you will know more about the limited investments that you have when it is time to let them go, and about the criteria you should use for choosing the investments that will replace them.

By understanding the investments in your portfolio, you will gain the wisdom and develop the restraint to hold them for the long term, to buy and sell intelligently according to your selected asset allocation, and to use your portfolio as an income generator and growth tool.

Types of Investments

At minimum, your portfolio should consist of three types of investments: stocks, exchange-traded funds, and bonds or income funds. A thoughtful combination of these investments will give you the opportunity to achieve growth, diversification, and income while saving you money usually lost through the internal expenses and commissions of loaded mutual funds and transaction costs charged by your broker-dealer.

Stocks. If you choose to have stocks in your portfolio, you must understand the nature of the investment that you have chosen. You will likely make more money by investing in individual equities, but if you do the holdings in your portfolio will be subject to larger fluctuations—up and down.

Picking stocks that fit your risk appetite, preferences, and values is no easy task. The stocks in your portfolio will be growth propellers and passive income generators, but they can also be a representation of your values, the world as you see it today, and what you hope for many years from now, including a world you may never see but your children and your community will inherit.

Recently, socially conscious investing has helped some investors critically analyze the types of companies they are considering for their portfolios. While you do not have to invest in socially conscious companies, knowing your criteria for investing makes picking stocks much easier for you and your advisor.

There are five simple but critical questions to ask yourself before adding a stock to your portfolio:

What does the company do? Understanding the company's function can lead to a deeper knowledge of how it makes a profit, its rank in its industry compared with competitors, if owning the stock could further diversify your holdings, and if there is an opportunity for growth in its industry.

Does the company make money? Numbers don't lie. A stock, no matter how trendy, is only as good as the money it makes through its operations. It comes down to earnings. Companies that have stable or growing earnings will, in most cases, see stable or higher stock prices over the long term.

What's the company's competitive advantage? When it comes to picking a stock, what gives it a *sufficient* competitive advantage over other companies of the same kind? This "moat," a term coined by Warren Buffett, acts as a defense against other companies that might try to enter the market.

How much of the stock do the company executives own? Executives' ownership stake in the company, shown in the amount of stock that they own, is a great indicator of the faith that they have in the company over the long haul and another great sign of whether to invest.

Does the stock diversify my portfolio? Less is more when less *does* more. Doubling up on similar investment types in your portfolio will only force your portfolio to react in one way in the face of a major market event. Choose investments from different industries, geographic locations, and risk levels, among other factors, to ensure that your portfolio mitigates the systematic risks of investing in the stock market.

Exchange-Traded Funds. If you don't want to go to the trouble of picking and investing in individual stocks, you can choose to invest in exchange-traded funds, a relatively new investment vehicle that has gained popularity because of its low cost and high efficiency.

Bonds. Bonds are great investments that provide fixed passive income. They have historically been sold as a risk-averse way for investors to earn interest on their principal. Bonds allow investors to help finance a company's operations with the expectation that the bondholder will be repaid a fixed amount at a defined interest rate and returned their principal amount at a date called the maturity date. You let a company borrow your money and they pay you back, with interest. Piece of cake.

While it is easy to understand the concept of bonds, they can be very hard to choose from—and like any other type of investment, they come with risks. For an individual bond, interest rates relative to the current interest rate environment can be an indicator of how risky the bond is (that is, the likelihood that the company you are investing in will default). The higher the interest rate on an individual bond, the higher the risk of your losing your principal. Bonds with such high yields/high risks are called junk bonds.

And if interest rates rise, your principal amount declines and changes the value of your bond. For this reason, you should focus on bonds with high ratings and intermediate maturity dates to mitigate the risk of the bond price changing drastically. This will allow you to keep up with changing interest rate environments and prevent you from being locked in to holding a depreciating asset.

Bonds also face inflation risks. Life will continually get more expensive, but will your fixed rate of return keep up? That is why overweighting bonds in your portfolio can limit its growth potential over time.

Annuities Versus Tax-Free Bonds. How do you spot a wolf in sheep's clothes? I'll give you a hint: He's probably trying to sell you an annuity. Annuities are high-commissioned, tax-deferred products that help an insurance sales-man cash in at your expense. Please, for your sake and for the sake of the generations to come, don't buy them. I'll tell you why. Annuities can act like traditional investment retirement accounts (like IRAs) in which you contribute money without limit to take advantage of the tax-deferred growth of your funds for retirement. At retirement, you are paid a designated amount on a basis selected by you, giving you a stream of income to last you through your golden years.

For the risk-averse, annuities are a lovely vehicle. They are sold as having no downside but an unlimited upside in the event of a *variable* annuity and with the added perk of peace of mind. But no. Annuities do way more damage than good. Between the ultra-high fees, fully taxable with-drawals, and contract penalties, there are enough reasons to look for other options.

Instead, choose tax-free bonds. You can invest in a bond of choice that will help a municipality, yield payments that are fully tax-free, provide income, and have no lockup limiting when you can sell the bond. The tax-free choice always wins.

◆ ◆ ◆

Hopefully, the desire to reach your goals will keep you committed to your plan through all market cycles. By con-tinually reassessing your risk tolerance and maintaining a portfolio of well-diversified growth holdings, you will be able to recover from any short-term market losses and

reap the benefits of your early and wise decision to get in
on the action.

STEP 4

MASTER MONEY DRAINS

The difference between death and taxes is death doesn't get worse every time Congress meets.

–Will Rogers

8

Control What
You Can Control

Mastering money drains is about thinking big, operating small, and pinpointing opportunities where you can control the outflow of money. Your focus needs to be on strategies to keep more of your money while playing the cards that you were dealt. You're going to lose money at some point along the way—that is inevitable. But here are seven ways you can control how much money you will lose.

Seven Simple Things You Can Control

Spending. Do you know that many of the minor leakages that hamper your plans happen after you have already been taxed? Yes! Your inability to budget can lead to serious and preventable money drains. But it doesn't have to be that way. As we discussed in Step 2, you must have a strong hold over your Master Budget. Knowing how much money you have coming in and how much is going out to fund things that you may not need could provide the answer to many of your problems. Always start here when you have the urge to analyze or complain about money drains. Turn back to the chapter 5 section on cash flow management goals for examples of easy (and not-so-easy) ways to cut back. This is the area you have the most power to do something about.

Investing. How you invest—and if you invest at all—matters greatly in terms of what portion of your income will go to taxes. (I'll dive into this in more detail in the next chapter.)

How You File Your Taxes. You can file your income tax return under one of five different tax statuses: single, married filing jointly, married filing separately, head of household, or qualifying widower or widower with a dependent. How you file has huge implications for your income tax payments. Talk to your accountant about the benefits of filing under one status versus another that may be available to you.

Itemizing Your Tax Deductions. In the world of income tax planning, itemizing is everything. Come tax time, you'll be asked to select either the itemized or standard deduction that the Internal Revenue Service (IRS) defines for you. The standard deduction may not account for all of the tax-deductible expenses you incur during a tax year and could be putting more money into the hands of the IRS. By itemizing deductions, you'll reduce your adjusted gross income—the measure that dictates your tax liability—and you'll save more money on your taxes.

Structuring Your Business. For the entrepreneurs out there, how you structure your business will have tax implications. Whether you own a sole proprietorship or a large corporation, the legal structure of your business will affect how much you pay in taxes. It is imperative to consult with legal and tax professionals on this matter.

Employing Contractors. Employees or contractors? Many business owners ask themselves this question when looking to scale their businesses. If you choose to employ individuals, you will have to deduct federal and state income taxes, FICA (Social Security) taxes, and Medicare taxes from your employees' salaries. These funds, called trusts, must be kept and paid periodically to the IRS. In addition, you'll be expected to match the FICA and Medicare amounts withheld from each employee's paycheck. Whoever said it costs to be the boss was not lying! Consider using contractors early on in your expansion to lower the tax liability that you will have for each employee. Running a business is difficult and expansion is sometimes the next step in developing your business. Knowing your business structure and needs could help save money while you're scaling up.

Using Professional Help. When all is said and done, make sure that more gets done than said. One way to ensure that you are putting all of the pieces together is by employing professional help—legal, tax, financial planning, and money management.

• • •

Controlling what you can control *is* the battle when you're managing money drains and their effects on your master plan. In the next chapter I explore the less intuitive ways you can use to curb outflows.

9

Two Birds, One Stone: Investment and Taxes

At this stage, you know what investment vehicles are staples for your portfolio and the different ways that you can use them to master income. But there is another pivotal piece to consider when investing in the capital markets: the tax implications. This chapter is about how to protect more of your hard-earned wealth through investing while still handling your civic duties.

Always Be Long Term

Your taxable investment accounts give you the opportunity to continue to make your money work for you outside of your retirement accounts. These accounts have no limit, but are subject to capital gains taxes depending on how long you hold the investments of your choice. These taxes can range as high as 20 percent on the net income made from the sale, but in many cases you can reduce the capital gains tax if you can hold on to an investment for longer than a year.

It pays to be patient and to think against the pull of your emotions. While an uptick in the value of investments in your taxable account may seem like something that you want to protect (by selling right away and netting the profit), the consequence of doing so may be unnecessary outflows. There will be special circumstances that warrant selling some of the securities in your portfolio. These reasons should be aligned with the goals of your master plan—for example, purchasing a home, sending your kids to school when the time comes, or using your investments for additional income in your later years. If your sights are truly set on the big picture, you must try to make all transactions long-term capital gains.

When Losses Work in Your Favor

The stock market is cyclical. As much as we want it to continue on a diagonal slope forever upward toward our goals, we have to recognize—not only through empirical data but through common sense—that what goes up must come down. At least with the stock market, we are assured by its performance history that what goes down will also go up again.

True Master Wealth-Builders look at downturns as opportunities. The commonly advertised opportunity is to buy stocks at a low price with the hope that the investment will appreciate when the stock market surges upward again. But this is only one way to take advantage of a fall in the market. There is another strategy that can help you in the more immediate future when you encounter a loss in investment value: tax loss harvesting.

Tax loss harvesting allows you to carry over losses from your investments to lower your tax liability. Here's how: You invested $10,000 and the market loses 10 percent over the course of the year. You sell your investment for a capital loss of $1,000. To the Internal Revenue Service, you have just lost $1,000 of ordinary income—even if you reinvest the $9,000 and experience an unrealized gain in the market. That $1,000 loss offsets your taxable income and reduces your tax liability. By reinvesting in a disciplined manner, you harvest your losses and save money in taxes. Not all losses are losses; some are gains in disguise. By working with a Certified Public Accountant you can more efficiently harvest your losses.

Why Retirement Accounts Matter for More Than Just Retirement

The days of the pension that delivers a hefty payment during your retirement years are gone—long gone. Social Security may not even be around when you retire in forty years or more. So that leaves your own retirement savings. The good thing is that your tax-deferred retirement account doesn't only pay for retirement, you can also use it to manage outflows.

When it comes to outflows, the biggest benefit of your tax-deferred employee-sponsored account is that your contributions lower your taxable income. You are accumulating funds for the expenses of tomorrow while saving on today's taxes! It is almost crazy how people don't get excited at this. I mean, really! You get to grow your money, you get free money from company matches, *and* you get a tax break by reducing your taxable income.

Fund your account, and then fund it some more. Whether it is a 401(k), 403(b), or a tax-deferred retirement account that you set up for yourself, take advantage by maxing out your accounts to save as much money as possible on your taxes during the tax year of contribution. It's a painless, effortless way to kill two birds with one stone: minimize tax outflows and set yourself up for a successful retirement.

Charitable Donations

Stocks. I love them—even if they sometimes come with capital gains taxes. Many organizations ask for cash donations for assistance with their nonprofit endeavors. But if you are thinking about diversifying the ways you give, I'd consider giving stock rather than cash.

Let's say you bought shares of Amazon (AMZN) worth $5,000 and they appreciated to $11,500. Instead of giving the charity $11,500 in cash, consider transferring the shares to your organization of choice. The benefit here is that you get the tax deduction for the gift of stock—but more important, you will not have to pay the capital gains tax for selling the stock because the cost basis (the original value of the stock when you bought it versus its current worth) will no longer apply. If the amount is big enough, this is a huge win for both you and the receiving charity.

◆ ◆ ◆

All of the strategies in this chapter provide you with ways to kill two birds with one stone—invest in something useful for your future while minimizing your current tax liability. If you take away just one thing from this chapter, please let it be this: Your investments and the decisions that you make regarding them should always serve multiple purposes.

MASTERING YOUR LEGACY

Someone is sitting in the shade today because someone planted a tree a long time ago.

–Warren Buffett

10

Your Personal Economy

It was one of the first springlike days in Washington, D.C., after a relatively mild winter. The cherry blossoms had appeared, temperatures were above eighty degrees, and the government was in full swing right before the upcoming recess. The town was buzzing and the hibernation from the winter months was officially at an end.

President Trump had just completed his first one hundred days in office, Congress had withdrawn the Republican healthcare bill prior to its scheduled vote, a new tax bill had just been introduced, and the stock market continued on an unusual rocketlike rise upward since the November 8, 2016, election. This gave the city a pulse—and a lot of subject matter to debate. Here I was, a young money manager caught in the middle of it all, stunned but invigorated.

Perhaps the most inspiring thing that happened in this period was meeting a man after a panel discussion that I moderated. Jim was a fellow Berkeley graduate with a lot of experience navigating the D.C. landscape. He was older but youthful, wise, and compassionate about the world around him. He ran the town, but he was humble enough to want to show other people how to succeed as well. He looked at his life as a chance to make the world and the people around him better.

We ate at Palm Restaurant in D.C., where the affluent met for lunch and mid-day wine before heading back to conquer the political jungle. Case in point: We were seated at a table next to Tucker Carlson, who was set to replace Bill O'Reilly on Fox News the following week. It was my first time there. At the table, Jim asked me about the book I was in the middle of writing (ahem, this book). I explained to him my four-step process for leveraging your youth for long-term financial wellness: master your mindset, master your plan, master your income, and master money drains.

I explained each of the segments and how they all added up to mastering your personal economy. There are two parts to your personal economy, I went on: the *economic* side, which incorporates your personal finances, and the *personal* side, which takes into consideration everything you value that money cannot buy. Our society's focus on the global economy and, quite frankly, the noise around us often leads us to forget the very things we can do to create the lives we want with what we already have. Our dreams, family, health, and hopes for the future are things that money can't buy but that enrich our lives in ways that money can never do. No government, rule, or regulation can accomplish this for us. It is all under our control, and our actions determine the legacy we leave behind.

I could see Jim mentally placing himself in each of the steps. He asked pointed and thoughtful questions about negative outflows, such as about his ownership interest in a racehorse and his use of real estate as a way of generating passive income. He had just one point to add: "Your personal economy will only understand your legacy based on what you do, not what you say."

In Jim's mind, how you approach your legacy was what would make or break a master plan. His words, like a light bulb, began to illuminate my mind with the different approaches to how you can master your personal economy.

Preparing Your Village

Everything is about you until everything *isn't* about you. At some point in life, you will become part of an interdependent village of people you care for deeply and who have helped sculpt the person you are. For example, in time many of us find ourselves running the wealth-building marathon race with our children and spouses and sometimes even our parents on our backs.

Currently, we are in the midst of the biggest transfer of wealth the country has ever seen. Thirty trillion dollars in wealth is being passed from Baby Boomers to their Gen X and Millennial children. Money, in amounts large and small, will be hitting the hands of people who may or may not be ready for it. Are you? Will your children be? While the financial well-being of your future generations may be the furthest thing from your mind right now, this last piece of the wealth-generation puzzle, mastering your personal economy, will become more and more obviously important as time marches on.

Your village is priceless. It is what makes the long and sometimes tedious wealth-building process worth it. You must give your village the right tools to build their own opportunities. Teaching your village through activity and example will ensure that they know what to do when money is in their hands and how to pass on those lessons to the next generation in turn. And the biggest example they will have when it comes to healthy money management practices is you. Your ability to master the plan will result in an inner circle of people who see money as a way to realize their own dreams.

A Seat at the Table

At the Palm Restaurant, Jim was not finished blessing me with his perspective on wealth generation. Jim's wife was Swedish and his family traveled frequently to Sweden. Jim seemed to have mastered just about everything about Swedish culture, from their preferences in alcohol to their tongue-twisting language. The man had it down pat. Through our playful banter, he dropped another gem.

"Whenever I go to Sweden, we cannot get together without bringing up my wife's mother. She will always have a seat at the table."

His wife's mother passed away many years ago, but her impact lingered on in the form of many memories, pho-

tographs, and family recipes. Her influence was powerful and distinctive. She was an example of how the Master Wealth-Builders in our lives and in our family lineage
never die. It wasn't the money she had earned or the steady
uptick in the value of her accounts that kept her ever-pres-
ent in her family's hearts and minds. It was not her creative business ideas. It was her investment in her village
and her commitment to giving the people she cared about
the opportunities to do more and be more.

Mastering your personal economy and building your
legacy is not just about dollars and cents. It requires creating an infrastructure that gives your people a seat at
the table, an opportunity to build for themselves. There
are people who have no idea what kinds of lives they
can build for themselves simply because they were never
given the opportunity. By contrast, there are families that
have known opportunity all their lives because someone
long ago had the audacity to try to build the life that they
imagined.

What you do today will influence the opportunities of
those that come after you and for those that follow them.
The hard truth is that some of their cards will be dealt
from your hand. This makes your actions critical to how
they can play the game. It starts with you. It starts now.

These four steps are intended to help you take the assets
you have now—plentiful or not—and multiply them over
the rest of your long lifetime so that you can create opportunities not only for yourself, but for the next iteration of
your village. And when your leg of the race is over, it is my
hope that people remember you for the person that you

were, not for the money you left them. It is my hope that what you *did* will be your legacy and that it will live on for many generations to come.

No matter who you are or whatever other resources you have, right now you have precious time. That is more than enough to start. And once you master what you do with your time, you will master your wealth. You will master your personal economy.

Afterword

You know, at one point I was worried—better yet, extremely terrified. It started in 2003 when my father, Lonbaye Yarnway, Sr., lost his battle to terminal prostate cancer. My world crumbled. As a kid in the inner-city streets of San Francisco, I now had to go from depending on my leader to leading myself. Experiencing this traumatic loss was my first, head-on experience with the reality of our mortality. Before his passing, I was already seen as the man of the house. When my dad had cardiac arrests, seizures, and complications from his chemotherapy, I was the one attending hospital visits and listening intently to the doctors. The paramedics would often turn to me to get information about his health. I lost my childhood. I lost the innocence that every child is born with. Then I lost my father.

There was some sunshine through those days, though. My dad, the traditional Liberian man, showed no weakness even though his blank eyes winced in pain. He shared stories and jokes and was the life of the party even as his life slowly slipped away. One of the best things that he did at this time was bringing my cousin Moses, whom I called my brother, over from Liberia. Already diagnosed with cancer, my father went to Liberia during a time of civil war. As the story goes, he was in the courtroom litigating for my brother's visa when gunshots rang out and bullets began whizzing through the air, almost killing them as they made their way to Roberts International Airport to depart for the United States. Years later that rush out of Liberia came to haunt my brother.

In January 2015, Moses became sick. He thought nothing of it. A common stomach flu, he thought. I was in Washington, D.C., at the time, growing my practice by going door-to-door to ask people whom I did not know to do business with me. Mo, as we called him, was my biggest fan. He'd routinely send me text messages to "keep going" and "don't quit," and would remind me that if anyone could do this it was me. In February, Mo was hospitalized due to complications from hepatitis B, which we later discovered had progressed into liver cancer, all because he had not been able to get a vaccine when escaping Liberia.

I slept in Dulles International Airport the night that Moses passed away. There was a blizzard in Virginia and all planes where grounded. In many ways, I feel as if God, the universe, or whomever you may believe in has spared me. Having my brother, my best friend, die might have broken me. Yet the memories that I have of him give me warmth and confidence to continue the work that I do for my family, for my trusting clients, and for myself.

From these experiences, I realized one thing: We are living on borrowed time. Every day, we are getting closer to other people assessing our legacies. We are living in a mad dash toward the end. *Young Money* is a money book that encourages you to use your time wisely, but doing so stretches far beyond money. My prayer for you is that it does not take the experiences that I have had to endure to get you to take action, but that this book serves as that call.

I look forward to seeing the great things you do with all that is in you.

Acknowledgments

Young Money could not have been possible without the help of a number of very important people. First and foremost, I'd like to thank God for the opportunity to write this book. My prayer is that it reaches the hands of all those with financial goals who need these exact words for their lives. I'd like to thank my mother, Tinniziee, for putting up with all of my shenanigans and the crazy ideas that I have about changing the world and building my firm. I appreciate your helping me to feel that my dreams are not so crazy at all. To my sister, Yousanie, who continues to be there when I need her and is one of the most inspiring people I've ever met. To Yantee, Leamon, Ernestine, and Plensah for being my biggest fans, whether near or far. To Shabnam, for reaching out to me with the idea of writing this book, I am forever grateful. To Danielle, for being a rock star of an editor—without you none of this would have been possible. Thank you for helping make my message stronger. To all of the clients who give me the privilege to serve them through Berknell Financial Group, I will always give you the best of me.

To my University of California, Berkeley, Sacred Heart Cathedral, and San Francisco Bay Area community, thank you for your unwavering support. To my fellow Liberians for exemplifying strength. To my fraternity, Alpha Phi Alpha and the divine nine for committing to the relentless fight for humanity. And, last but not least, to you, for reading this book and designing a beautiful life.

Index

About the Author

Dasarte Yarnway is founder and managing director of Berknell Financial Group (BFG), a fiduciary wealth management and financial planning firm headquartered in San Francisco, California. Born in San Francisco and raised in that city's Geneva  Towers housing project, Dasarte's curiosity about money and the way it works began when he saw the lack of money in his community's households, schools, and businesses. His own parents were Liberian immigrants who had been forced to leave their country because of the threat of civil war. In response to these experiences, he sought to create the multigenerational wealth that his family and the families around his neighborhood lacked.

From community organizing and service to youth mentorship, Dasarte has dedicated his life to helping people find freedom through their financial decisions. His Advice With You In Mind motto and movement has inspired many to think about finances in a way that allows them to live out their wildest dreams.

Berknell Financial Group, established in 2015, currently has three offices, in San Francisco, Seattle, and Washington, D.C. By using its RIITE planning process, BFG advisors seek to help their clients reach their goals in the areas of retirement planning, investments, insurance, and taxes and estate planning without conflict of interest. Dasarte plans on expanding the firm to help change the narrative and the experience of investors and their financial advisors for the better.

Berrett–Koehler
Publishers

Berrett-Koehler is an independent publisher dedicated to an ambitious mission: *Connecting people and ideas to create a world that works for all.*

We believe that the solutions to the world's problems will come from all of us, working at all levels: in our organizations, in our society, and in our own lives. Our BK Business books help people make their organizations more humane, democratic, diverse, and effective (we don't think there's any contradiction there). Our BK Currents books offer pathways to creating a more just, equitable, and sustainable society. Our BK Life books help people create positive change in their lives and align their personal practices with their aspirations for a better world.

All of our books are designed to bring people seeking positive change together around the ideas that empower them to see and shape the world in a new way.

And we strive to practice what we preach. At the core of our approach is Stewardship, a deep sense of responsibility to administer the company for the benefit of all of our stakeholder groups including authors, customers, employees, investors, service providers, and the communities and environment around us. Everything we do is built around this and our other key values of quality, partnership, inclusion, and sustainability.

This is why we are both a B-Corporation and a California Benefit Corporation—a certification and a for-profit legal status that require us to adhere to the highest standards for corporate, social, and environmental performance.

We are grateful to our readers, authors, and other friends of the company who consider themselves to be part of the BK Community. We hope that you, too, will join us in our mission.

A BK Life Book

BK Life books help people clarify and align their values, aspirations, and actions. Whether you want to manage your time more effectively or uncover your true purpose, these books are designed to instigate infectious positive change that starts with you. Make your mark!

To find out more, visit **www.bkconnection.com**.

Berrett–Koehler
Publishers

Connecting people and ideas
to create a world that works for all

Dear Reader,

Thank you for picking up this book and joining our worldwide community of Berrett-Koehler readers. We share ideas that bring positive change into people's lives, organizations, and society.

To welcome you, we'd like to offer you a free e-book. You can pick from among twelve of our bestselling books by entering the promotional code **BKP92E** here: http://www.bkconnection.com/welcome.

When you claim your free e-book, we'll also send you a copy of our e-newsletter, the *BK Communiqué*. Although you're free to unsubscribe, there are many benefits to sticking around. In every issue of our newsletter you'll find

- A free e-book
- Tips from famous authors
- Discounts on spotlight titles
- Hilarious insider publishing news
- A chance to win a prize for answering a riddle

Best of all, our readers tell us, "Your newsletter is the only one I actually read." So claim your gift today, and please stay in touch!

Sincerely,

Charlotte Ashlock
Steward of the BK Website

Questions? Comments? Contact me at bkcommunity@bkpub.com.

Certified
B Corporation
bcorporation.net